"More than ever we need Jung, whose intuitions are proving indispensable to understanding and interacting with the twentyfirst century, from issues of globalism and ecological crisis, to the challenges of living with technology. *C.G. Jung: the Basics* offers excellent starting points for complete beginners or for those seeking fresh psychological perspectives on history, modernity, symbolism, spirituality, the arts, creative practice and our relationships to each other and the planet. Suitable for clinicians in training and students of disciplines from the humanities to the social sciences, this book brings an important resource into accessible and exciting perspective for our times."

– **Susan Rowland, PhD**, is Chair of MA Engaged Humanities and the Creative Life at Pacifica Graduate Institute, and teaches on the doctoral program in Jungian psychology and Archetypal Studies. She is the author of *Remembering Dionysus: Revisioning Psychology and Literature in C. G. Jung and James Hillman* (Routledge 2017)

"The basics are the essential facts or principles of a subject. This is what Ruth Williams has brilliantly given us in relation to the work of C.G. Jung, analytical psychology, Jungian analysis and Jungian studies. Her book is accessible, beautifully structured and presented. She really knows her way around the Jungian world and can play the role of guide with consummate ease."

– From the Foreword by Andrew Samuels, Professor of Analytical Psychology, University of Essex

"Ruth Williams discusses the unconscious, the structure of the psyche, the archetypes, and individuation, as well as psychological types, dreams, alchemy, and the vexed question of Jung's political engagement in a way that will, I hope, encourage the reader to look more closely at what Jung has to offer us in the twenty-first century. There are many different ways in which to approach Jung: through his indebtedness to German culture, for instance, or through applying his conceptual tools in the field of literary criticism or film studies, or through studying the institutional development of analytical psychology and the personalities involved in the Jungian movement. What is valuable about the account offered in this book is that it provides an overview of the 'basics' of Jungian thought in a way that is both helpful and clear. Jung once described the second part of Goethe's *Faust* as 'a link in the *aurea catena*' — i.e., the Golden or Homeric Chain — 'which has existed from the beginnings of philosophical alchemy and Gnosticism down to Nietzsche's *Zarathustra*'; in engaging with this material Jung found that it was 'unpopular, ambiguous, and dangerous', and he believed he had embarked on 'a voyage of discovery to the other pole of the world'. As one embarks on one's own journey into Jung, it is good to have a guide such as this in one's hands."

— **Paul Bishop**, William Jacks Chair of Modern Languages
at the University of Glasgow, UK; co-editor of
The Ecstatic and the Archaic (Routledge)

C.G. JUNG

THE BASICS

C.G. Jung: The Basics is an accessible, concise introduction to the life and ideas of C.G. Jung for readers of all backgrounds, from those new to Jung's work to those looking for a convenient reference.

Ruth Williams eloquently and succinctly introduces the key concepts of Jungian theory and paints his biographical picture with clarity. The book begins with an overview of Jung's family life, childhood, and relationship with (and subsequent split from) Sigmund Freud. Williams then progresses thematically through the key concepts in his work, clearly explaining ideas including the unconscious, the structure of the psyche, archetypes, individuation, psychological types and alchemy. *C.G. Jung: The Basics* also presents Jung's theories on dreams and the self, and explains how his ideas developed and how they can be applied to everyday life. The book also discusses some of the negative claims made about Jung, especially his ideas on politics, race and gender, and includes detailed explanations and examples throughout, including a chronology of Jung's life and suggested further reading.

C.G. Jung: The Basics will be key reading for students at all levels coming to Jung's ideas for the first time and general readers with an interest in his work. For those already familiar with Jungian concepts, it will provide a helpful guide to applying these ideas to the real world.

Ruth Williams is a Jungian Analyst, Professional Member and Supervising Analyst with the Association of Jungian Analysts in London, UK. She has been in clinical practice for more than 25 years. Her website can be found at www.ruthwilliams.org.uk.

THE BASICS SERIES

For a full list of titles in this series, please visit www.routledge.com/The-Basics/book-series/B

ROMAN CATHOLICISM (SECOND EDITION)
MICHAEL WALSH

SEMIOTICS (SECOND EDITION)
DANIEL CHANDLER

SHAKESPEARE (THIRD EDITION)
SEAN MCEVOY

SOCIAL AND LABOUR MARKET POLICY
BENT GREVE

SOCIAL WORK
MARK DOEL

SOCIOLOGY (SECOND EDITION)
KEN PLUMMER

SPECIAL EDUCATIONAL NEEDS AND DISABILITY (SECOND EDITION)
JANICE WEARMOUTH

SPORT MANAGEMENT
ROBERT WILSON AND MARK PIEKARZ

SPORT PSYCHOLOGY
DAVID TOD

SPORTS COACHING
LAURA PURDY

STANISLAVSKI
ROSE WHYMAN

SUBCULTURES
ROSS HAENFLER

SUSTAINABILITY
PETER JACQUES

TELEVISION STUDIES
TOBY MILLER

TERRORISM
JAMES LUTZ AND BRENDA LUTZ

THEATRE STUDIES (SECOND EDITION)
ROBERT LEACH

TRANSLATION
JULIANE HOUSE

WITCHCRAFT
MARION GIBSON

WOMEN'S STUDIES
BONNIE SMITH

WORLD HISTORY
PETER N. STEARNS

WORLD THEATRE
E. J. WESTLAKE

RESEARCH METHODS
NICHOLAS WALLIMAN

CONTEMPORARY INDIA
REKHA DATTA

GENDER (SECOND EDITION)
HILARY M. LIPS

C.G. JUNG
THE BASICS

Ruth Williams

Routledge
Taylor & Francis Group

LONDON AND NEW YORK

First published 2019
by Routledge
2 Park Square, Milton Park, Abingdon, Oxon OX14 4RN

and by Routledge
52 Vanderbilt Avenue, New York, NY 10017

Routledge is an imprint of the Taylor & Francis Group, an informa business

British Library Cataloguing in Publication Data
A catalogue record for this book is available from the British Library

Library of Congress Cataloging in Publication Data
Names: Williams, Ruth, 1956 August 15– author.
Title: C. G. Jung : the basics / Ruth Williams.
Description: 1 Edition. | New York : Routledge, 2019. |
Series: The basics | Includes bibliographical references.
Identifiers: LCCN 2018035012 (print) | LCCN 2018036514 (ebook) |
ISBN 9781315638416 (Master Ebook) | ISBN 9781317270966 (Abode Reader) |
ISBN 9781317270959 (Epub) | ISBN 9781317270942 (Mobipocket) |
ISBN 9781138195424 (hardback) | ISBN 9781138195448 (pbk.) |
ISBN 9781315638416 (ebk)
Subjects: LCSH: Jung, C. G. (Carl Gustav), 1875–1961. | Psychoanalysis.
Classification: LCC BF109.J8 (ebook) | LCC BF109.J8 W555 2019 (print) |
DDC 150.19/5–dc23
LC record available at https://lccn.loc.gov/2018035012

ISBN: 978-1-138-19542-4 (hbk)
ISBN: 978-1-138-19544-8 (pbk)
ISBN: 978-1-315-63841-6 (ebk)

Typeset in Bembo
by Out of House Publishing

-A=io

CONTENTS

A NOTE ON REFERENCES

References to the Collected Works of C.G. Jung are made by year of first publication followed by the paragraph number in the *Collected Works*.

ACKNOWLEDGEMENTS

Heartfelt thanks are due to all the patients who so graciously gave permission for extracts from their work to be published. Thank you.

Thanks to Professor Andrew Samuels for agreeing to write a Foreword and for your staunch care and support throughout all the years.

My thanks to Antonia Boll for permission to quote from her unpublished paper in Chapter 1.

Thank you to Dr Dale Mathers for kindly reading and commenting on Chapters 1, 4, 5, 6 and 7, which greatly enhanced the writing.

Thank you to Dr Claire Asherson Bartram for reading and giving helpful feedback on Chapters 3 and 7.

Thanks to Jack Bierschenk for kindly reading and giving me helpful feedback on Chapter 3.

Thanks to Jessica Woolliscroft for her constructive and helpful feedback on the Introduction and Chapter 3.

Deep appreciation and respect to the artist Rosemary Woolliscroft who so generously created the art for the book cover.

Sincere thanks to Susannah Frearson of Routledge for her sensitive, creative and helpful support throughout. And to all the staff at Routledge who have made the creation of this book such a satisfying experience.

Thank you to all the patients, teachers and friends who have taught me all I know and made this book possible.

Profound gratitude to the guiding forces of creativity who inspired me throughout to go beyond anywhere I knew was possible. Called or not....

And to the spirit of C.G. Jung without whom there would be no book – thank you.

Responsibility for any errors is of course my own.

PERMISSIONS

ILLUSTRATIONS

FOREWORD
Andrew Samuels

The word 'basic' is very interesting. On the one hand, if something functions as a base then it is a foundation or a safe place from which to venture into a potentially difficult world. On the other hand, base metals are regarded as inferior to gold and silver, and base can mean lowly or inferior. What opposites! Usually, though, the basics are the essential facts or principles of a subject. This is what Ruth Williams has brilliantly given us in relation to the work of C.G. Jung, analytical psychology, Jungian analysis and Jungian Studies.

Ruth Williams brings dual qualifications to her task. She has qualified as a Jungian analyst and also in Jungian Studies at postgraduate level. As important, she really knows her way around the Jungian world and can play the role of guide with consummate ease. Her book is accessible, beautifully structured and presented, and – more quietly – takes a stand against the manualisation and medicalisation of psychology, psychotherapy and counselling. So there is also discussion of the kinds of Western societies that prevail today.

When I trained as a Jungian analyst 46 years ago, I could never have imagined that Jungian ideas and approaches would be offered at undergraduate level in universities all over the world. Yet the literature simply has not kept up with this and, without mincing words, it is clear that the books and papers students are asked to read are way beyond them (though not denying that, in time, things will become clearer and more comprehensible). In this regard, as in many others, Freudian psychoanalysis has paid greater attention to the communication of its basics than have the Jungians. Not anymore!

This book will be essential reading on the undergraduate courses just mentioned, as well as courses in the same area at Masters level. This is because students doing their Masters in Jungian Studies, in my experience, simply start out of the blue in the majority of cases. Yes, they are postgraduate – but, being honest, what does that mean? They need a book like this just as much as do undergraduates.

Then there are psychotherapists and counsellors whose course is not officially 'Jungian' but in which Jungian ideas are definitely part of the core curriculum. What are these budding clinicians supposed to read? Most so-called introductory texts in the Jung area are written in such an uncritical spirit that it is hard to imagine them really turning on trainees and candidates who do not absolutely have to study Jungian material.

What about people undergoing Jungian analytical and psychotherapeutic training? Surely this book will be beneath them? I beg to disagree. The merging of responsible explanation with a well-informed critical edge is a highly positive feature of *Jung: The Basics*.

And there is another potentially seminal role for the book in the Jungian world. Right now, considerable attention is being given to producing a more integrative approach within Jungian psychology. Up until now, the official Jungian trainings have operated in tribal silos. What is missing – and provided by this lucid and succinct work, is some kind of core document that points towards a more unified Jungian field. In addition, this is not at all a 'British' book. The author is abreast of international developments and a global readership is assured.

To the amazement I recorded earlier that there are now undergraduate and Masters courses on Jung, I would add that there has been an unexpected explosion in the study of Jungian ideas in the academy. This is taking place in the arts and humanities, religious studies, and even in the social sciences. One outstanding subject area is cinema and film studies, which has, to an extent, put Freud, Lacan and Laplanche behind itself and has turned to Jungian and post-Jungian perspectives.

I mentioned earlier the twin spectres of manualisation and med-icalisation in relation to psychotherapy today. Students need to be introduced to today's battle for the soul. When the press is full of the praises of Cognitive Behavioural Therapy, despite either the critiques of the spurious yet supportive research, or the evidence in favour of deeper therapies, isn't it important that students get a space to think for themselves about this? But they cannot do that in a vacuum and this is where the book comes in.

I'll turn now to a couple of problems that face the Jungian 'brand' these days. The first is that Freud is the altogether bigger and better-known thinker. Of course, Freud has his immensely powerful critics as well. But when I ask Masters students in the psychoanalysis areas to give their spontaneous word associations to the word 'Jung', they invariably come up with the word 'Freud'! I think that there are sev-eral reasons for this. One is that there is a market-style competition going on. Another, though, is that there is a dearth of information coming from the Jungian side.

The second problem is that Jung has attracted a reputation for being particularly prejudiced, more than the norm for his times. This applies to anti-Semitism, racial hierarchies, sexism, homophobia, and a general social and cultural elitism. The fact is there is something to be concerned about – as there is with many if not all thinkers of such standing. So the shadows over Jung cannot be wished away – and Ruth Williams does not get into a PR exercise. But what she has to say is balanced and stimulating. One can so easily imagine students and their lecturers engaging with passion on these aspects of Jung, using the book as a starting point.

Finally, I want to answer the question that has bedevilled the entry of Jungian ideas into university teaching. "Won't the students take it all personally?" Well, yes, they will. And maybe they should for, in Jung's words, "every psychology is a personal confession". Students who think it is all about them need to be reminded by staff self-disclosure that it is all about them – the staff – too!

London, April 2018
Andrew Samuels is Professor of Analytical Psychology
at the University of Essex, and a Training Analyst of
the Society of Analytical Psychology, London.
www.andrewsamuels.com

TABLE 00.1 C.G. Jung: The Basics. Table setting out the timeline of Jung's life including biographical and historical key points.

1875	Carl Gustav Jung born 26 July in Kesswil, Switzerland.	
1895–1900	Attends Basel University to study science and medicine.	
1900	Specialises in psychiatry.	
1902–3	Attends Salpetrière Hospital in Paris to study with Pierre Janet.	**Quotes Freud as authority**
1903	Marries Emma Rauschenbach on 14 February. (Five children: Agathe Niehus, Gret Baumann, Franz Jung-Merker, Marianne Niehus, Helene Hoerni.)	
1903–5	Begins voluntary work at Burghölzli Clinic in Zurich under Professor Eugen Bleuler where he develops his Word Association tests.	
1905–13	Lecturer on medical faculty at Zurich University.	
1906	Begins corresponding with Freud.	
1907	First meeting with Freud in Vienna lasting 13 hours.	
1909	**The beginning of Jung's 'psychoanalytic period', which lasts until 1913.** Leaves Burghölzli. Sets up in private practice. Travels with Freud and Ferenczi to guest lecture at Clark University in the United States where he is awarded an honorary degree.	
1910	Lectures at Fordham University in New York where he is awarded an honorary doctorate.	

1913	Jung introduces the term 'Analytical Psychology'.	
1914	**Intermediate period 1914–20** December 1913 Jung starts his work on what became Active Imagination and *The Red Book*.	**World War I**
1918	Begins to study gnosticism	
1922	**Mature 'Analytic' period when his own concepts were defined.**	
1923	His mother dies.	
1928	Begins to study alchemy.	
1932	Prize for Literature, City of Zurich.	
1933	Beginning of Eranos conferences.	
1935	Tavistock Lectures in London.	
1936	Lectures at Harvard where he is awarded an honarary doctorate.	
1937	Terry Lectures at Yale.	
1937–8	Honorary doctorates awarded by universities of Calcutta, Benares and Allahabad.	
1938	Honorary doctorate from Oxford University.	
1939	Honorary Member of the Royal Society of Medicine, London.	**World War II**
1944	Stops university teaching after heart attack.	

(*Continued*)

(Continued)

1945	Honorary doctorate from Geneva University.	
1948	C.G. Jung Institute in Zurich founded.	
1951	Publishes work on synchronicity.	
1953	Collected Works published.	
1955	Honorary doctorate by Swiss Technological Institute. Emma Jung dies.	
1960	Named honorary citizen of Küssnacht.	
1961	Jung dies 6 June, Küssnacht.	

This table is based on the chronology of Jung's Life and Work in *Carl Gustav Jung: Critical Assessments* (Ed. Papadopoulos), London and New York: Routledge, 1992.

PREFACE

The idea behind this book is that you can dip in and out, reading each chapter as the mood takes you. There is no narrative running through the book from beginning to end which needs to be followed, although the order of the chapters makes sense in terms of building an understanding of the material. It is written so as to be accessible to a general reader who does not necessarily have any previous knowledge of Jung, although it is hoped that it will be of interest to those who have had some contact with his ideas too.

You might want to bear in mind the following line from Kafka as you read:

> The correct perception of any matter and a complete misunderstanding of the matter do not completely exclude one another.
>
> (quoted in Samuels 1989 p.225)

So do not despair if things don't make sense immediately!

The writing in this book is deliberately styled at points as an interlocution. This encourages you to bring your own subjectivity to the reading, to think about the ideas as they might relate to you personally. This particularly applies to the chapters on dreams and psychological types, in that we all dream (even if we do not remember them), and many of us would be curious to work out our psychological type and think about the ramifications.

Clinical practitioners are known as Jungian analysts, or Analytical Psychologists (the term adopted to differentiate Jungian psychology from psychoanalysis). Some have reclaimed that title and refer to Jungian psychoanalysis.

INTRODUCTION

It has to be acknowledged at the outset that Jung is not an easy read. His *Collected Works* stretch to over 20 volumes and he ranges widely to draw in obscure figures, shifts into Classical languages at the drop of a hat, and assumes we have knowledge of obscure myths and ideas, which to be honest most of us do not (at least not without looking them up!). There are times when I have resorted to using a light pencil line to cross out vast swathes of Jung's writing where he goes off on long tangents riffing on obscure subjects, so as to keep a sense of the precise point he is making. (Please don't take this as encouragement to deface books!) He does come back to the point. Jung had a mind like a rich tapestry. Sometimes it helps to pick out one colour at a time to follow the thread.

A good starting point in approaching Jung is to read what is sometimes called Jung's autobiography, *Memories, Dreams, Reflections* (Jaffé 1963), which Jung wrote in collaboration with Aniela Jaffé and which was published posthumously. It was an extraordinary life, both inner and outer, and his 'autobiography' gives a real sense of the man. There are biographies which might be of interest too (Bair 2003, McLynn 1996, Stevens 1994, von Franz 1975).

A second step might be to turn to *Man and His Symbols* (Jung 1964), which contains chapters written by Jung as well as some of his closest colleagues and covers the key aspects in Jung's psychology. It was written during the last year of Jung's life and was intended to reach a wide, non-specialist readership. He was encouraged to write this volume by John Freeman who interviewed Jung in 1959 for the BBC 'Face to Face' series, which is accessible via online resources. The interview contains the now famous interchange whereby Freeman asks Jung if he believes in God. Jung's reply: "I don't need to believe. I know". (It should be noted this is said with confidence; not arrogance.)

There are a number of anthologies of work by contemporary analysts which provide a modern take on Jung's ideas. Excellent examples are *The Handbook of Jungian Psychology* (Papadopoulos (Ed.) 2006), and a collection of reflections by eminent Jungians on how and why we still read Jung in the 21st century (Kirsch & Stein 2013).

A personal account of his own journey towards becoming a Jungian and the texts he found most helpful can be found in Thomas B. Kirsch (2013) who not only grew up the son of two Jungian analysts who had both been in analysis with Jung, but he too had the opportunity to consult with Jung personally. So Kirsch has a unique tale to tell about his personal encounter with Jung and Jungian psychology.

Two further volumes would also be of value to the reader seeking their way into Jung. The first is *The Quotable Jung* (Harris 2016), which is a selection of key passages from Jung's *oeuvre* and the second is *The Critical Dictionary of Jungian Analysis* (Samuels *et al* 1986), which I have liberally turned to throughout the writing of this book.

The professional world of Jungian analysis is worldwide and there is an International Association for Analytical Psychology (https://iaap.org/) with over 3,000 analyst members. There are some key hubs of activity where there are large numbers of Jungians working today: Zurich (Jung's hometown), London, New York, San Francisco. There are many Jungians in South America and there are developing groups in China, India, Russia, Ukraine and all over Eastern Europe. While much of the literature referenced in this book hails from the main hubs, I have made a point of including writers from all over the world. Jung's ideas are applicable to us irrespective of culture or creed. We may all find our own way into his ideas and take out what we find relevant.

There are international Jungian journals which attract scholars from around the world to contribute in a dialogue to take Jung's pioneering ideas forward and make them relevant today.

Also, a few academic institutions offer distance learning to those wishing to explore Jung in such a context (see 'Further study').

BIOGRAPHICAL DETAIL

Carl Gustav Jung (1873–1961) was the first surviving son of a country parson in Switzerland whom he found disappointing, and an unhappy, unstable mother. The families of both Jung's parents were poor although professional and well respected. The parents were both the thirteenth child in their respective families, which was seen as a good omen (Bair 2003 p.7).

Carl Gustav Jung the elder (1794–1864) – Jung's grandfather – became a highly sought-after physician in Basel, was rector of the university, Grand Master of the Swiss Freemasons and wrote both scientific treatises as well as theatrical plays. As is often the case, perhaps Jung had more in common with his grandfather than his own father. Jung the elder was rumoured to be the illegitimate son of Goethe. Johann Wolfgang von Goethe (1749–1832), considered the most important German literary figure in modern times, was the author of *Faust* (1998[1808]).

Jung's maternal grandparents were equally striking. Samuel Preiswerk (1799–1871) was a senior figure in the church. He is said to have had spiritual visions and conversed with the dead. Indeed, several members of the family were said to have had psychic abilities.

Helène Preiswerk, Jung's cousin, was involved in mediumistic experiments which became the subject of Jung's medical dissertation of 1902.

Jung's relationship with both his parents was – as with all of us – pivotal. He was sorely disappointed with his father whose faith he saw as by rote rather than something spiritually alive and meaningful. So perhaps this was a spur which led Jung to such depths and heights of spiritual exploration as can be seen in his writings. His mother's state of mind became something he had to surmount. She was besieged by ghosts and apparitions. He saw her as having two distinct personalities: the daytime and night-time mothers. In his early life she left the family on several occasions to go into a rest home and the feeling of the feminine became something he associated with "natural unreliability", which Jung came to call the "handicap" from which his attitudes towards women were formed (Bair 2003 pp. 20–21). (More of Jung's relationship with the feminine in Chapters 3 and 8.)

Jung married Emma Rauschenbach on Valentine's Day in 1903. She was a fabulously wealthy heiress with her own family ghost stories. She enabled Jung to fulfil his ambitions and transcend his more modest background. Emma became a psychoanalyst in her own right and wrote some important works, notably *The Grail Legend* (1998) written in collaboration with Marie-Louise von Franz (1915–98), one of Jung's closest colleagues.

Jung and his family lived in Küsnacht, Switzerland in an elegant home which Jung had built on what was known as the gold coast on the lake-side in Zurich and where he entertained the likes of Albert Einstein (Nobel Prize-winning physicist 1879–1936). Jung also had a tower built at nearby Bollingen, which was his refuge where he went to introspect and create. He deliberately had no running water or electricity at the tower so it was like 'going back to nature'. He would spend time there building fires on which to cook, writing and meditating.

While to some Jung was – and perhaps is – seen as a mystic or visionary, he was always keen to see himself as an empirical scientist. His writing demonstrates both sides of this nature.

People travelled from all over the world, especially America, to consult with Jung in Zurich. A 'Jung Club' was established where people gathered for lectures on Jungian thought. Clubs have since sprung up across the world.

In his lifetime Jung achieved every success in terms of family, wealth, honour and professional accolades.

PROFESSIONAL LIFE

Having become a psychiatrist (which at the time had no status), Jung joined the staff of the Burghölzli Psychiatric Hospital in Zurich on 10 December 1900, where he lived a fairly monastic life, working long hours under Professor Eugen Bleuler who imposed a teetotal regime on staff. This was somewhat at odds with Jung's nature as he was quite a gourmand. While working at the Burghölzli, Jung developed his Word Association Test (described in Chapter 3).

During his time working at the Burghölzli, Jung met and treated Sabina Spielrein (1885–1942) who went on to become an analyst in her own right. She wrote a paper (1912) which was to prove instrumental in Freud's development of a death instinct. She has been somewhat marginalised in the history of depth psychology although in recent years efforts have been made to reinstate her as someone of note rather than the subject of lurid speculation (Covington & Wharton 2003). Spielrein was analyst to Jean Piaget (1896–1980), who was a pioneer in the field of child development. It was on the subject of Sabina Spielrein that Jung first approached Freud, which led to their subsequent collaboration as colleagues.

By the time of his appointment to the Burghölzli, Jung had already begun reading Sigmund Freud including *The Interpretation of Dreams* (1953), which he described in the obituary he wrote for Freud (1939) as epoch-making and:

> probably the boldest attempt that has ever been made to master the riddles of the unconscious psyche... For us, then young psychiatrists, it was... a source of illumination, while for our older colleagues it was an object of mockery.
>
> (Jaffé 1963 p.169, n.2)

The two men – Jung and Freud – finally met when Jung and his wife visited Vienna in February 1907. There was an immediate rapport between the men and their first conversation famously lasted 13 hours without a pause. Initially Freud saw Jung as his heir apparent and treated him like a prince. But this was not to last. They travelled to the United States together in 1909 to lecture at Clark University. During the sailing they both analysed each other's dreams. Jung had an important dream on the voyage (set out in Chapter 6), which he decided he could not be honest about because he was by now convinced Freud's thinking was too limited to grasp the meaning which Jung intuited for himself. This was a crux point between the two of them. Their relationship began to hit the buffers when in 1910 Freud said to Jung:

> Promise me never to abandon the sexual theory. That is the most essential thing of all. You see we must make a dogma of it, an unshakeable bulwark.... against the black tide... of occultism.
>
> (Jaffé 1963 p.173)

This went to the heart of their differences. So that, when Jung published *The Psychology of the Unconscious* (1912) (which was later revised and renamed *Symbols of Transformation* [1956]), their differences became naked. Jung's take on *libido* had a broader span as he saw libido as not something purely sexual, but rather as energy in a larger sense encompassing the spiritual; this proved to be a decisive difference.

The relationship ended in a sad exchange of letters dated January 1913 when Freud wrote:

> I propose that we abandon our personal relations entirely. I shall lose nothing by it, for my only emotional tie with you has long been a thin thread.
>
> (McGuire (Ed.) 1974 p.539)

Jung replied:

> I accede to your wish that we abandon our personal relations, for I never thrust my friendship on anyone. You yourself are the best judge of what this moment means for you. "The rest is silence".
>
> (ibid. p.540)

The quote is from Shakespeare's Hamlet Act 5, scene 2.

Canadian psychiatrist Henri Ellenberger (1905–93) in his encyclopaedic volume (1970) sees the problem between the two as fundamental differences in philosophical approach. They are both grounded in the period known as Romanticism, which was a movement in the late 18th century in arts and literature putting inspiration, subjectivity, and the primacy of the individual at the heart of matters. Further:

> whereas Freud's aim is to explore that part of the human mind that was known intuitively by the great writers, Jung claims to have approached objectively and annexed to sciences a realm of the human soul intermediate between religion and psychology.
>
> (Ellenberger 1970 p.657)

While most people automatically link Jung and Freud and see Jung as creating an offshoot of psychoanalysis, Sonu Shamdasani (Professor and Jung historian at University College, London) regards this as a "complete dislocation of Jung and complex psychology in the intellectual history of the twentieth century" (2003 p.13). He suggests Jung's earlier and more significant influences included Pierre Janet (1859–1947) in Paris and others.

Jung was ahead of his time in many ways. He was a believer in interdisciplinary projects, which led him to working collaboratively across a range of disciplines such as with Karl Kerenyi (1897–1973) (expert in Greek mythology); with Nobel Laureate Wolfgang Pauli (1900–58), pioneer of quantum physics on the interface between physics and depth psychology; and with Richard Wilhelm (discussed in Chapter 3) on Chinese alchemy and the *I Ching*.

Jung's interests spanned all manner of esoterica from gnosticism, alchemy, the *I Ching*, astrology, and the paranormal. He even wrote about flying saucers (1958)! (In fact the paper is not as whacky as it might sound and it has been useful in clinical practice.) He had a substantial library containing volumes on every conceivable subject (Shamdasani 2011).

SYMBOLIC LIFE

While Jung lived a fairly traditional family and professional life, and conformed to societal norms leading an upper-middle-class lifestyle, he was at the same time steeped in an inner world of dreams, creativity and imagery which guided him. This was particularly the case during the period around 1913–18 when he underwent a deep process of transformation (discussed in Chapter 4) which led him to his most authentic and original discoveries. He had to contend with the most challenging experiences, which some saw as a psychotic episode. I do not go along with that notion since even during that time he was able to continue his professional practice and functioned well. Please see the table of works published during this period on page xxxi.

NEW AGE

During the 1960s and 1970s the term *New Age* sprang up to describe the rapid changes taking place in the Western world whereby many were adopting a new approach to spirituality to circumvent religious dogma. Central to *New Age* thinking is the belief that self-awareness and God-awareness are indistinguishable and that God can be found within (Greene 2018 p.152). (This idea is developed in Chapter 2). There are those who see this thinking in pejorative terms, seeing it as a 'pick and mix' approach lacking the discipline or rigour of religion.

Jung became something of a guru to some people in the *New Age* who saw his independent approach as inspirational. It was apparent Jung had not approached religion 'off the shelf' but underwent his

TABLE 0.1 Works written/published during the period 1913–18

CW Volume	Title	Year
3	The Content of the Psychoses	1914(n1)
3	On Psychological Understanding	1914
3	On the Importance of Unconscious Psychopathology	1914
4	The Theory of Psychoanalysis	1913(n2)
4	General Aspects of Psychoanalysis	1913
4	Psychoanalysis and Neurosis	1916
	Some Crucial Points in Psychoanalysis: A Correspondence between Dr Jung and Dr Loy	1914
4	Prefaces to "Collected Papers on Analytical Psychology"	1916
6	A Contribution to the Study of Psychological Types	1913
7	The Psychology of the Unconscious	1917
7	The Structure of the Unconscious	1916
8	The Transcendent Function	1916(n3)
8	Instinct and Unconscious	1919(n4)
8	General Aspects of Dream Psychology	1916(n5)
10	The Role of the Unconscious	1918

Notes:

n1. Delivered as a lecture in 1908. Second augmented edition 1914.

n2. Delivered as a lecture in 1912.

n3. Written in 1916; published 1958.

n4. Written in 1919. Published with a short concluding note in 1948.

n5. Twice expanded and published in CW version 1948.

own profound journey of self-discovery. Jungian academic David Tacey in Australia has written about Jung and the so-called *New Age* (2001).

In fact, the *New Age* really begins earlier. It is linked to what is called the *Age of Aquarius*, which began as far back as the 18th century. Others believe it is yet to begin even if the stirrings are already present. Jung has been credited with being the first person to disseminate the idea that the New Age would be Aquarian (Greene 2018 p.157).

Jung encourages us to seek wholeness; not perfection. Far from the *laisser faire* 'let it all hang out' attitude which can at times be attributed to *New Age* thinking, Jung actually saw this shift as quite ominous. He sees the signs:

> pointing in this direction consist in the fact that the cosmic power of self-destruction is given into the hands of man and that man inherits the dual nature of the Father. He will [mis]understand it and he will be tempted to ruin the universal life of the earth.
>
> (Jung letter to Victor White, 10 April 1954
> in *C.G. Jung Letters*, Vol. 2, p.167)

In the age of Trump and Brexit; of ideological extremism, corporate globalisation, despoliation of the planet and threats being made to nuclear powers, this is a sobering thought. This attitude helps to ground the *New Age* perspective, which could otherwise be seen as too one-sided and up in the air.

LEGACY

There is a thriving population of Jungians in the 21st century in terms of clinicians, academic researchers and general interest in the wider public. Indeed it could be said, where Freudian thinking dominated the 20th century, that Jung's time has come in the 21st century. The publication of Jung's *The Red Book* (2009) attracted massive media interest and the original was on display at the Venice Biennale, a prestigious art and cultural event founded in 1895.

There is a burgeoning field of Jungian film studies which looks at film through a Jungian lens in interesting and creative ways. In particular, Jung's theory of archetypes has been adopted in film-making to assist in concocting powerful storylines and characters in an attempt to draw on the numinosity (spiritual quality and power) associated with archetypes (discussed fully in Chapter 3), as if there were a neat formula to successful storytelling.

Jung is more popular in humanities departments (the academic discipline concerned with culture and society as opposed to hard sciences where things can be 'proved' literally) than psychology departments. Some interesting examples of this are Rowland (Ed.) (2008), which is a collection of essays on Jungian approaches to the arts in myriad forms, as well her 2017 volume or her highly original work on Jung's writing style (2005), which may be of use in grappling with his convoluted, sometimes chaotic way of writing. Rowland sees the very style as communicating something profound about the material and the processes he was describing. He writes in a way he describes as circumambulating the text, which means that he approaches an issue from various angles as if walking around the subject to get different perspectives. Susan Rowland is Chair of the Engaged Humanities and the Creative Life MA at Pacifica Graduate Institute in California, and prior to that was a Professor of English and Post-Jungian Studies at the University of Greenwich in the UK. She has a unique take on Jung.

Some of Jung's ideas have entered the mainstream: synchronicity, introversion-extraversion, complexes and more. Although Jung is presently less of a force in the Western Academy than Freud, he is in the culture: he appeared on the album cover of The Beatles' *Sgt Pepper's Lonely Hearts Club Band* (1967), analysed German novelist Hermann Hesse (1877–1962), influenced David Bowie who makes various references to Jung in his *Aladdin Sane* album (1973) (a play on 'a lad insane'); inspired the award-winning album by 'The Police' entitled *Synchronicity* (1983); was instrumental in introducing mysticism to the West and an early influence on the ideas behind Alcoholics Anonymous.

"Summoned or not, the gods will be there" was the motto from the Oracle at Delphi, which Jung had carved in Latin above his front door. You might experience this as an angel on your shoulder, or an inner guide, or even luck being on your side. Sometimes you might wake with a start with a dream image or thought. Catching these moments can be like finding gold dust. "There are gods, gods everywhere, and nowhere left to put my feet" said the 12th-century poet and philosopher Basava (quoted in Beard 2018, p.119).

In Jung's *Red Book* (Chapter 4) he refers to the spirit of the times and the spirit of the depths. I would like to invoke the following idea at the beginning of this book as an attitude to adopt in reading Jung:

> The way forward is inward, downward, to a radical engagement with the powers of imagination. This is the way Jung took as he followed the "spirit of the depths" in his day. This way is still available today for the courageous individual.
>
> (Stein 2017 p.11)

Perhaps a good guiding principle for life.

If it did not have relevance today as a living experience, Jung's psychology would become an anachronistic albeit interesting historical set of ideas. Jung shows us by example how to undertake a spiritual quest and live a life more aligned with our 'purpose'. The journey is not simply intellectual. It is an inner journey too:

> The knowledge of the heart is in no book and is not to be found in the mouth of any teacher, but grows out of you like a green seed from the dark earth... But how can I attain the knowledge of the heart? You attain this knowledge only by living your life to the full. You live your life fully if you also live what you have never lived, but left for others to live or to think.
> (Jung, *The Red Book, Liber Primus*, fol. ii(r)/ii(v), p.233)

REFERENCES

Bair, D. (2003) *Jung: A Biography*. Boston, MA: Little Brown.

Beard, M. (2018) *How Do We Look? The Eye of Faith*. London: Profile Books.

Bowie, D. (1973) *Aladdin Sane*. RCA Records.

Covington, C. & Wharton, B. (2003) *Sabina Spielrein: Forgotten Pioneer of Psychoanalysis*. Hove & New York: Brunner-Routledge.

Ellenberger, H. F. (1970) *The Discovery of the Unconscious: The History and Evolution of Dynamic Psychiatry*. New York: Basic Books.

von Franz, M-L. (1975) *C.G. Jung: His Myth in Our Time*. New York: G.P. Putnam's Sons.

Freud, S. (1953) "The Interpretation of Dreams" in *The Standard Edition of the Complete Psychological Works of Sigmund Freud* (Tr. J. Strachey, Vol. 4). London: Hogarth Press.

von Goethe, J.W. (1998 [1808]) *Faust: Part 1*. Oxford World's Classics. Oxford & New York: Oxford University Press.

Greene, L. (2018) *Jung's Studies in Astrology: Prophecy, Magic and the Qualities of Time*. London & New York: Routledge.

Harris, J. (2016) *The Quotable Jung*. (Collected and edited by Judith Harris with the collaboration of Tony Woolfson). Princeton, NJ: Princeton University Press.

Jaffé, A. (1963) *Memories, Dreams, Reflections*. London: Fontana Press, 1995.

Jung, C.G. (1912) *The Psychology of the Unconscious: A Study of the Transformations and Symbolisms of the Libido. A Contribution to the History of the Evolution of Thought*. London: Kegan, Paul, Trench, Trubner, 1933.

Jung, C.G. (1913–30) (Ed. S. Shamdasani; Tr. M. Kyburz, J. Peck & S. Shamdasani). *The Red Book: Liber Novus*. London: W.W. Norton, 2009.

Jung, C.G. (1956) *Symbols of Transformation*, CW 5.

Jung, C.G. (1958) "Flying Saucers: A Modern Myth of Things Seen in the Skies" in CW 10.

Jung, C.G. (1964) *Man and His Symbols*. London: Picador, 1978.

Jung, C.G. (1976) *C.G. Jung Letters. Vol. 2*. (Ed. G. Adler & A. Jaffé; Trans. R.F.C. Hull). London: Routledge & Kegan Paul.

Jung, E. & von Franz, M-L. (1998) *The Grail Legend*. Princeton, NJ: Princeton University Press.

Kirsch, J. & Stein, M. (Eds.) (2013) *How and Why We Still Read Jung: Personal and Professional Reflections*. London & New York: Routledge.

Kirsch, T. B. (2013) "A Lifelong Reading of Jung" in *How and Why We Still Read Jung: Personal and Professional Reflections*. (Ed. J. Kirsch & M. Stein). London & New York: Routledge. pp. 195–209.

McGuire, W. (Ed.) (1974) *The Freud/Jung Letters*. (Trans. R. Manheim & R.F.C. Hull). London: Hogarth Press and Routledge & Kegan Paul.

McLynn, F. (1996) *Carl Gustav Jung: A Biography*. London: Black Swan, 1997.

Papadopoulos, R. (2006) *Handbook of Jungian Psychology*. London & New York: Routledge.

Rowland S. (2005) *Jung as a Writer*. Hove & New York: Routledge.

Rowland, S. (Ed.) (2008) *Psyche and the Arts: Jungian Approaches to Music, Architecture, Literature, Painting and Film*. Hove & New York: Routledge.

Rowland, S. (2010) *C.G. Jung in the Humanities: Taking the Soul's Path*. New Orleans, LA: Spring Journal Books.

Samuels, A. (1989) *The Plural Psyche: Personality, Morality and the Father*. London & New York: Routledge.

Samuels, A, Shorter, B. & Plaut, F. (1986) *A Critical Dictionary of Jungian Analysis*. London & New York: Routledge.

Shamdasani, S. (2003) *Jung and the Making of Modern Psychology: The Dream of a Science*. Cambridge: Cambridge University Press.

Shamdasani, S. (2011) *C. G. Jung: A Biography in Books*. New York & London: W. W. Norton & Company.

Spielrein, S. (1912) "Destruction as the Cause of Coming into Being" in *Journal of Analytical Psychology* Vol. 39 No. 2. pp. 155–186, 1994.

Stein, M. (2017) "Introduction" to *Jung's Red Book For Our Time: Searching for Soul under Postmodern Conditions* (Eds. M. Stein & T. Arzt). Asheville, NC: Chiron Publications.

Stevens, A. (1994) *Jung* (Past Masters Series). Oxford: Oxford Paperbacks.

Tacey, D. (2001) *Jung and the New Age*. Abingdon & New York: Brunner-Routledge.

The Beatles (1967) *Sgt Pepper's Lonely Hearts Club Band*. Apple/Parlophone/EMI.

The Police (1983) *Synchronicity*. A&M.

♂ In the centre, the white light, shining in the firmament; in the first circle, protoplasmic life-seeds; in the second, rotating cosmic principles which contain the four primary colours; in the third and fourth. creative forces working inward and outward. At the cardinal points, the masculine and feminine souls, both again divided into light and dark

Mandala 105 from Jung's *Red Book*, which also appears as Plate A6 in Volume 13 of the *Collected Works*. Reprinted with kind permission of W.W. Norton

1

THE UNCONSCIOUS

ATTITUDE

To approach the subject of the unconscious requires a mind open to unknown possibilities. It is a difficult idea to conceptualise as it seems at first to be talking about an absence of something, consciousness in this case. It may seem as if we are chasing something invisible. Well – at the risk of talking in riddles – it is invisible, but may be discerned. To explain. There are fundamental features of life which are invisible such as air and gravity, yet they exert indisputable influence over our existence. Gravity was 'discovered' when Newton made the mental leap to realise gravity could be inferred. He saw the apple drop and understood the implications – there must be some force drawing the apple to the ground.

In the same way, we can infer the presence of the unconscious by reference to parapraxes (usually called Freudian slips), and by analysing dreams (the manifestation *par excellence* of unconscious processes) and referring backwards to see something dynamic was at play. It may initially help to suspend judgement about what the unconscious is and whether it exists; to maintain an agnostic stance. What is required might be something akin to what poet John Keats (1795–1821) called 'negative capability', which conveys the idea that a person's potential can be defined by what he or she does *not* possess. I am invoking this idea in the spirit of allowing what is mysterious or unknown to remain hanging in the air as a possibility.

A helpful metaphor for the unconscious utilised by writer Hermann Hesse (1877–1962) in *Steppenwolf* (1972 pp.192–209) would be the way the theatre stage at any given instant, like a dream or the unconscious, might be seen as encompassing everything – the cast waiting to come on, the backstage crew, the audience, the writer, and so on.

HISTORY

Let's briefly look at how and when the unconscious was first discovered.

The earliest figures are Gustav Fechner (1801–87), who is regarded as the founder of experimental psychology, followed by Theodore Lipps (1851–1914), both of whom gave the unconscious "a place of decisive importance" (Jung 1954, par. 354). Although it was philosopher Christian von Wolff (1679–1754) who was the first to speak of 'empirical' or 'experimental' psychology (in his *Psychologia empirica of 1732*) (ibid. par. 345 and n4). Wilhelm Wundt (1832–1920), also acclaimed as a founding father of experimental psychology, taught the first course in psychology in 1862. His *Principles of Physiological Psychology* was first published in Leipzig in 1893. The psychological treatment of neuroses was pioneered by Jean-Martin Charcot (1825–93) at the Salpetrière Hospital in Paris, and Pierre Janet (1859–1947), also based in Paris (who published *L'Automatisme psychologique* in Paris in 1889, followed by *Néuroses et idées fixes* in 1898). At around the same time Hippolyte Bernheim in Nancy was working in the area of treating neuroses by suggestion by following in the footsteps of A.A. Liébeault. They both published works in 1866, with Bernheim's being translated from French to German by Sigmund Freud, who was apparently greatly inspired by Bernheim's work and laid the foundations for his own project. Central Europe was in a ferment of creativity in this area of exploration during this period. (This was also the case in terms of art and furniture-making and creativity in a much broader sense, which is beyond the scope of this volume.) Both Freud and Jung went to the roots of this movement to study, Jung to work with Janet, and Freud with Charcot.

In 1902 William James (1842–1910), American psychologist and philosopher (the brother of novelist Henry James), wrote:

> I cannot but think that the most important step forward that has occurred in psychology since I have been a student of that science is the discovery, first made in 1886, that ... there is not only the consciousness of the ordinary field, with its usual center and margin, but an addition thereto in the shape of a set of memories, thoughts, and feelings which are extramarginal and outside of the primary consciousness altogether, but yet must be classed as conscious facts of some sort, able to reveal their presence by unmistakable signs.
>
> (1982 p.233)

The discovery in 1886 to which he refers is the positing of a "subliminal consciousness" by Frederick W.H. Myers (see n23 in Jung 1954 par. 356), a pioneer of parapsychology, the study of 'occult' phenomena and spiritualism.

WHAT IS THE UNCONSCIOUS?

I am deliberately avoiding discussing the subject of consciousness at depth as it would require an entire volume. While consciousness may be seen as encompassing simple awareness of the objects around us in a very literal way all the way up to spiritual awakening and development, likewise unconsciousness can stretch from a simple lack of awareness of something, to a dense unknowing or unknowable sense, which is the stuff of the psychological unconscious I will be referring to. I would emphasise that there is no negative judgement implied in something being *un*conscious. Indeed many things *must* remain unconscious or we would be utterly overwhelmed by a welter of data. Jung:

> [T]he unconscious depicts an extremely fluid state of affairs: everything of which I know, but of which I am not at the moment thinking; everything of which I was once conscious but have now forgotten; everything perceived by my senses, but not noted by my conscious mind; everything which, involuntarily and without paying attention to it, I feel, think, remember, want and do; all the future things that are taking shape in me and will sometime come to consciousness; all this is the content of the unconscious.
>
> (1954 par. 382)

PSYCHOID UNCONSCIOUS

Jung then adds: "We must also include in the unconscious the psychoid functions that are not capable of consciousness and of whose existence we have only indirect knowledge" (ibid.). Jung first posited the notion of a psychoid unconscious, completely inaccessible to consciousness, in 1946. This is where things start to get more complicated. He went on to link this to the idea of the *unus mundus*, or 'one world', in which everything is connected on a subtle level, which may initially seem irrational. It relates to the unitary nature of reality beyond the Cartesian split between mind and body. This gives us a framework to understand the uncanny experiences we all have from time to time such as ringing someone at the moment they are calling you, intuiting someone's intention so you 'know' what they are feeling; even feeling an unexplained affinity for someone. In much the same way telephone wires – or WiFi waves nowadays – connect us all from whatever physical distance, we may think about this idea of the 'one world' as invisibly connecting us. This has been conceptualised in a variety of ways. Jung calls the *unus mundus* a "metaphysical speculation" (1944 par. 660), a theory which helps us think about something so intangible. The psychoid archetype/ unconscious:

> has a tendency to behave as though it were not located in one person but were active in the whole environment. The fact or situation is transmitted in most cases through a subliminal perception of the affect it produces.... As soon as the dialogue between two people touches on something fundamental, essential, and numinous, and a certain rapport is felt, it gives rise to a phenomenon which Lévy-Bruhl fittingly called *participation mystique*. It is an unconscious identity in which two individual psychic spheres interpenetrate to such a degree that it is impossible to say what belongs to whom.
>
> (Jung 1958 par. 851–2)

Jung here provides a theoretical framework to understand the existence of a non-duality which many of us intuit. We have uncanny experiences but had no previous way of making sense of them. This has found great appeal among New Age thinkers.

Similar notions of interconnectedness and wholeness may be found in the ideas of Rupert Sheldrake when he writes about fields of 'morphic resonance' (2009) (discussed below); in Laszlo (2004), who refers to the Akashic field (*Akasha* being the Sanskrit word for ether which is added to the other four elements: earth, fire, water, air); and in Bohm (1980) who talks of an implicate order. David Bohm (1917–92) was a pioneering theoretical physicist and a former protegé of Albert Einstein. These are all deep ideas that warrant exploration.

SYNCHRONICITY

Jung located the psychoid archetype

> beyond the psychic sphere, analogous to the position of the physiological instinct, which is immediately rooted in the stuff of the organism and... forms the bridge to matter in general
>
> (1954 par. 420)

One might say it is where psyche and matter meet. Main encapsulates the complexity when he suggests the concepts:

> of psyche and matter and space and time merge into a psychophysical space-time continuum... To express this ambivalent nature – at once psychic and physical yet neither because beyond both – [Jung] was led to coin the term 'psychoid'.
>
> (1997 p.36)

Jung sees the psychoid as possessing parapsychological qualities which he groups with synchronicity. Synchronicity is probably one of the features of Jung's thought which has become most widely known. It refers to the coming together of two or more events for which a rational explanation does not exist. Jung referred to this phenomenon as being acausal. Jung's formulation – even discovery – of synchronicity (which he first posited in 1928) has always been at the edge of scientific understanding. Developing these ideas in discussions with Nobel Laureates Albert Einstein (1879–1955) and pioneer of quantum physics Wolfgang Pauli (1900–58), Jung found the principle "bore parallels to certain discoveries in relativity theory and quantum mechanics" (Tarnas 2006 p.50). Richard Tarnas is Professor of Philosophy and Psychology at the California Institute of Integral Studies, having previously served as Esalen's director of programs and education. (Esalen was established in the 1960s as a counter-culture centre of the Human Potential movement.) Main goes further, seeing synchronicity and the psychoid factor as "helping to bring about a rapprochement between psychology and physics" (1997 p.19). "The dramatic coincidence of meaning between an inner state and a simultaneous external event", Tarnas concludes, "seemed to bring forth in the individual a healing movement towards psychological wholeness, mediated by the unexpected integration of inner and outer realities" (2006 pp.50–51). This carries with it a sense of meaning to an otherwise random event. Jung accordingly referred to synchronicity as an "acausal connecting principle" (1952). Cambray gives us a sense of the grandeur of this idea:

> Jung is speaking ... about acausal coincident phenomena that are meaningfully linked, but the collapse of space and time together with the disappearance of the principle of causality is remarkably congruent with the best theories in physics for the origins of the universe. The point in this is to try and articulate what Jung may be reaching for with his theory of synchronicity. It is as if at the deepest level he is finding a place for the psyche at the origins of the universe through the psychoid archetype. This is not an intelligent design argument but an indication that the universe is permeated with psyche as it is with space, time and matter; that synchronicities provide the traces of an original undifferentiated state. In such a cosmogony I suggest Jung is leading us to see psyche as another of the potentials inherent in the singularity.

(2009 p.20)

These radical ideas challenge traditional Western scientific thought. They make us stop and think.

In "Psychological Commentary on the Tibetan Book of the Great Liberation" in which Jung contrasts Eastern and Western modes of thinking, he elaborates (before he has formally theorised the psychoid unconscious) the linked nature of 'one mind':

> The statement 'Nor is one's own mind separable from other minds' is another way of expressing the fact of 'all contamination'. Since all distinctions vanish in the unconscious condition, it is only logical that the distinction between separate minds should disappear too.

(1939 [1958] par. 817)

There are several theories which map ways in which we can understand the deep connection both between ourselves and with the earth and nature (see discussion of Ecopsychology in Chapter 8). To clarify matters, I will give three examples of synchronicities:

The first is a snippet from clinical work. I was told a dream in a session with a client which concerned five coins. After the session, on going out at lunchtime, I came upon five coins in the street outside my consulting room. I initially saw one, then the next, began laughing to myself and thought "there are going to be five of these!" and of course... there they were. It was very striking – an unexplainable enigma. It would be great to be able to relate how it was then possible in a further session to go on to make meaning of this, but unfortunately this did not happen. However, its uncanny nature conveyed a sense of meaning and significance which might otherwise have been absent and this experience remains vivid many years later. Synchronicity conveys a sense of meaning to otherwise random events. It is not mere serendipity.

The second example is from Jung's clinical practice. He discusses the case of a rather intellectual young woman who appeared unreachable. He thought he needed to wait for a random event to occur to break the impasse. As Jung was listening to this woman in session one day, she reported the following:

> She had had an impressive dream the night before, in which someone had given her a golden scarab – a costly piece of jewellery. While she was still telling me this dream, I heard something behind me gently tapping on the window. I turned round and saw that it was a fairly large flying insect that was knocking against the window-pane from outside in the obvious effort to get into the dark room. This seemed to me very strange. I opened the window immediately and caught the insect in the air as it flew in. It was a scarabaeid beetle ... whose gold-green colour most nearly resembles that of a golden scarab. I handed the beetle to my patient with the words, "Here is your scarab." This experience punctured the desired hole in her rationalism and broke the ice of her intellectual resistance. The treatment could now be continued with satisfactory results.

(1951 par. 982)

The recounting of the dream and the appearance of the scarab were simultaneous. There is no rational explanation for this 'coincidence', but the fact they occurred simultaneously creates a link and the uncanny experience, which is often associated with synchronicities. The consequent shift in the woman's disposition may be seen as more than a random change such as might occur with a shock. The nature of this synchronicity enabled her to proceed with a newly acquired attitude. At the least it shook her out of her rational thinking as what occurred was so striking. Interestingly, the scarab beetle – associated with the god Khepri in Egyptian mythology – is a symbol of creation and rebirth. We could think metaphorically in terms of this synchronicity bringing about a metaphorical rebirth in terms of the woman's shift from stuckness. The appearance of the scarab at the window in Jung's office might be seen as a kind of spontaneous creation (birth) of a powerful symbol which proved so helpful.

A final example is from a work by Roderick Main (Professor of Analytical Psychology at the University of Essex and a world authority on synchronicity):

> An analyst on vacation suddenly had a strong visual impression of one of her patients she knew to be suicidal. Unable to account for the impression as having arisen by any normal chain of mental associations, she immediately sent a telegram telling the patient not to do anything foolish. Two days later she learned that, just before the telegram arrived, the patient had gone into the kitchen and turned on the gas valve with the intention of killing herself. Startled by the postman ringing the doorbell, she turned the valve off; and even more struck by the content of the telegram he delivered, she did not resume her attempt.
>
> (von Franz 1992 pp.24–25 quoted in
> Main 2007 pp.1–2)

FUNCTION OF THE UNCONSCIOUS

Things also become interesting when you can begin to understand that there is a purposive function to the unconscious. You can explore this by becoming adept at noticing and interpreting the modes of expression through which the unconscious makes itself known: imagery and symbolism which may appear in dreams or, in waking life, in the form of fantasies, desires and synchronicities. The unconscious may also be spotted as emotional expectations, hopes and prejudices.

Jung developed a method he called Active Imagination to deliberately invoke the process (see Chapter 4) of encouraging the unfolding of unconscious fantasies. It should be emphasised that this does not necessarily mean that the contents of the unconscious will be a desired discovery. The contents may indeed be unwanted – see Chapter 2 for discussion of what Jung called the Shadow.

SUMMARY

We have sketched out the pioneers of psychology and a psychological approach to working with neuroses who were early influences on both Jung and Freud. We have looked at the discovery of the unconscious, its history, nature, function and connection to synchronicity. The major theoretical speculations on the interconnectedness of the universe have been mentioned in connection with the psychoid unconscious and synchronicity.

JUNG'S WRITINGS

Jung's Collected Works runs to 20 volumes plus a number of supplementary volumes transcribing series of seminars on dreams, visions and other subjects (see 'Further reading'). (There is a project underway to publish Jung's complete writings which will probably double the output.) He was a prolific writer and much of it concerns his approach to the unconscious. Table 1.1 sets out his principal published writings on the unconscious in the Collected Works:

JUNG'S MODEL OF THE UNCONSCIOUS

The defining feature of Jung's thinking about the unconscious is he saw its structure as having two parts: a personal unconscious, as well as a collective unconscious which he saw as the repository of universal motifs – or archetypes – that give rise to ideas and symbols across cultures and time. (See Chapter 3 for a full discussion of archetypes). This second category is unique to Jung. Contemporary Jungian analyst in Santa Fé, New Mexico, Jerome Bernstein, describes

TABLE 1.1 Jung's principal writings on the unconscious

Date	Vol.	Paras.	Title
1912	4	314–39	The Fantasies of the Unconscious
1914	3	438–65	On the Importance of the Unconscious in Psychopathology
1917	7	266–95	The Function of the Unconscious
1917	7	192–200	General Remarks on the Therapeutic Approach to the Unconscious
1917	7	1–201	On the Psychology of the Unconscious
1917	7	221–42	Phenomena Resulting from the Assimilation of the Unconscious
1917	7	451–63	Phenomena Resulting from the Assimilation of the Unconscious
1917	7	202–406	The Relations between the Ego and the Unconscious
1917	7	442–521	The Structure of the Unconscious
1917	7	341–73	The Technique of Differentiation between the Ego and the Figures in the Unconscious
1917	7	141–91	The Archetypes of the Collective Unconscious
1917	7	97–120	The Personal and the Collective (or Transpersonal) Unconscious
1917	7	202–65	The Effect of the Unconscious upon Consciousness
1917	7	442–50	The Distinction between the Personal and Impersonal Unconscious
1917	7	202–20	The Personal and the Collective Unconscious
1918	10	1–48	The Role of the Unconscious
1919	8	263–82	Instinct and the Unconscious
1920	6	568–76	The Attitude of the Unconscious
1920	6	626–7	General Description of the Types
1932	18	1223–5	The Hypothesis of the Collective Unconscious
1936/7	9i	87–110	The Concept of the Collective Unconscious
1937	11	1–55	The Autonomy of the Unconscious
1939	9i	489–524	Conscious, Unconscious and Individuation
1942	13	210–12	The Rapprochment with the Unconscious
1944	12	516–17	The Unconscious as the Matrix of Symbols
1947	8	356–64	The Significance of the Unconscious in Psychology

Date	Vol.	Paras.	Title
1952	11	449–67	Foreward to White's God and the Unconscious
1954	13	463–82	The Interpretation and Integration of the Unconscious
1954	8	343–55	The Unconscious in Historical Perspective
1954	9i	whole	The Archetypes and the Collective Unconscious
1954	9i	1–86	Archetypes of the Collective Unconscious
1954	8	381–7	Conscious and Unconscious
1954	8	388–96	The Unconscious as a Multiple Conciousness
1961	18	444–60	The Functions of the Unconscious (from Man and His Symbols)

the discovery of the collective unconscious as being perhaps one of Jung's most brilliant contributions, of the order of Freud's 'discovery' of the personal unconscious (2005 p.72).

The unconscious is never inactive. It is constantly sifting unconscious elements. The unconscious is seen as compensating the conscious attitude to adjust one's way of thinking/perceiving with a fuller 'deck of cards'. What becomes more fully conscious is to some extent predicated by the strength of a person's ego (discussed more fully in Chapter 2); it has to be capable of being handled. The process of becoming more conscious is seen as life-enhancing. Perhaps you have sometimes felt life is teaching you lessons – offering awareness, putting opportunities in your path? These may be construed as a creative dialogue with a spiritual meaning, giving a sense of purpose to life and the 'problems' we encounter. It sometimes seems as if we are given choices which would take life in different directions. (See also Chapter 4 on Individuation.) This is the idea behind the film *Sliding Doors* (Dir: Peter Howitt, 1998) starring Gwyneth Paltrow, which illustrates the parallel lives that may be lived if a different choice is made. What if?

PERSONAL UNCONSCIOUS

The contents of the personal unconscious are acquired during one's lifetime and evolve even during infancy. They are ordinarily out of awareness. These would include aspects of oneself which are pushed into the background and which feel unwanted; characteristics with which one does not like to be associated; feelings which are too difficult to express or which currently feel inappropriate or impossible to articulate. Feelings, thoughts, intuitions can be buried. Others recede into the background without our conscious will.

COLLECTIVE UNCONSCIOUS

As Jung began to differentiate his ideas from Freud, he had a dream. This helped him formulate the idea of a collective unconscious, which was without precedent. The dream is quoted in full:

> I was in a house I did not know, which had two storeys. It was "my house". I found myself in the upper storey, where there was a kind of salon furnished with fine old pieces in rococo style. On the walls hung a number of precious old paintings. I wondered that this should be my house, and thought, "Not bad." But then it occurred to me that I did not know what the lower floor looked like. Descending the stairs, I reached the ground floor. There everything was much older, and I realised that this part of the house must date from about the fifteenth or sixteenth century. The furnishings were medieval; the floors were of red brick. Everywhere it was rather dark. I went from one room to another, thinking, "Now I really must explore the whole house". I came upon a heavy door, and opened it. Beyond it, I discovered a stone stairway that led down into the cellar. Descending again, I found myself in a beautifully vaulted room which looked extremely ancient. Examining the walls, I discovered layers of brick among the ordinary stone blocks, and chips of brick in the mortar. As soon as I saw this I knew that the walls dated from Roman times. My interest by now was intense. I looked more closely at the floor. It was of stone slabs, and in one of these I discovered a ring. When I pulled it, the stone slab lifted, and again I saw a stairway of narrow stone steps leading down into the depths. These, too, I descended, and entered a low cave cut into the rock. Thick dust lay on the floor, and in the dust were scattered bones and broken pottery, like remains of a primitive culture. I discovered two human skulls, obviously very old and half disintegrated.

(1963 pp.182–3)

Do take time to read the dream carefully. It was pivotal for Jung both in terms of formulating his own ideas, and differentiating them from

Freud. The image of the dream house going back to older and older periods was clearly evocative and inspirational. It encapsulated ideas which Jung went on to develop. He saw our minds as being built of ever more ancient layers to which we can gain access. Some believe we can reconnect with past lives but that is beyond the scope of Jungian thought.

Jung's dream took place on a voyage to America which he undertook with Freud when they were both invited to lecture at Clark University in 1909. During the journey they shared dreams with each other and mutually analysed them. However, Jung found himself increasingly disappointed by what he regarded as Freud's limited perspective. When they discussed the dream cited, he dissembled and found himself fabricating a version to fit in with Freud's wish-fulfilment theory even though Jung knew this was inadequate. It was clear to Jung that the dream house represented an image of the psyche going back to increasingly archaic levels of consciousness. He saw it as a structural diagram, intimating an impersonal – or collective – layer of consciousness.

The collective unconscious is made up of archetypes (discussed in greater detail in Chapter 3).

... AND THE BODY

A contemporary aspect of thinking about the unconscious concerns psychosomatic illness. The term is common parlance indicating a connection between mind and body, used to understand how physical illness, or psychological illness, can become embedded in the body. This is conceptualised by Jung in terms of the psychoid unconscious (see above). These concepts help us understand intergenerational transmission of traumatic events: matters experienced by one person pass down through a family or community and produce symptoms, which may only then be assimilated or healed. This may sound a little far-fetched, so I give some examples. The British psychoanalyst Joyce McDougall writes about this in her book entitled *Theatres of the Body* (1989): the physical body 'carries' a trauma/sickness/communication which cannot be otherwise expressed. She discusses a patient whom she called Georgette who found it reassuring to be ill as, when she was most besieged by physical pain, "this brought in its wake a feeling of comfort and relief from the mental suffering" (1989 p.141). Georgette was anorexic during her childhood and adolescence; and contracted bronchial asthma from a young age. In later life she had gastric ulcers and crippling rheumatic pains. She further developed what she described as frightening tachycardia, which she thought of as probably being an hysterical manifestation connected to her father's death from a heart attack. The litany continued (in the words of the patient quoted in McDougall):

> I have a number of skin allergies. Cat fur makes me itch all over, and some foods ... make me swell up. Uriticaria and more serious reactions. (She went on to develop symptoms resembling Quincke's edema and added that when this was localized in her throat it was frightening.)... I inherited these allergies from my mother. She sometimes had to be hospitalized because of the violence of her reactions. Whenever my skin itched or swelled up she would say "you're just like me."
>
> (ibid. p.147)

This was connected to a feeling of being engulfed by her mother so she felt as if she did not exist as an individual. This in turn meant she could continue to feel connected to her mother psychologically instead of experiencing the loss of separation as she became an independent adult. As the analysis progressed, the symptoms petered out, which created a further level of anxiety. The patient: "If I no longer get asthma or catch colds or continue to create ulcers, it's as though I no longer exist" (ibid. p.152). You can see how the symptoms have a meaningful function for this patient in the absence of being able to think things through.

A further vignette from clinical practice:

Rosalind was the younger of two daughters of a Holocaust survivor who left her native Vienna on the Kindertransport (a train bringing Jewish children to Britain, leaving their parents behind in Nazi-occupied Germany and Austria with the likelihood they would never meet again). The children were naturally traumatised by this experience. They were housed with strangers; many were treated like maids. They made their way as best they could and indeed many went on to lead successful lives and had families of their own. Most did not open up about their early experiences and as a consequence (by which I imply no blame) the trauma has been passed on down through the generations. There are now fourth-generation 'survivors' (ie great grandchildren of the original Holocaust survivors) who are left to deal with the consequences of these events. In Rosalind's case she was turned into the family's black sheep and become physically ill to such an extent that, over the course of the two-year family dispute, she touched death four times. This was alarming, something she had to deal with separately from her family – itself a repeat of the situation her mother had experienced. Simplistically, this is how disturbance can unconsciously find its way into the body and create symptoms. There is a growing body of literature beginning to build on this subject as the second- and third-generation survivors begin to write about their experiences (see for example, Salberg and Grand 2017 and Grand and Salberg 2017).

A connected but separate aspect of the body and the unconscious is a phenomenon which therapists/analysts refer to as bodily countertransference by which they 'pick up' feelings from a patient in their body, who communicate to the therapist/analyst things which cannot be put into words. This is wholly unconscious. Indeed, it cannot be replicated in a conscious way. The therapist/analyst's body acts as a tuning fork (referred to in Stone 2006) by which they are able to resonate with what is being communicated. This is a component of empathy which helps the therapist/analyst to both understand the patient and to find a way of communicating that so the patient feels understood.

IN FILM AND ART

At its best, art will produce material which stems from the unconscious. It naturally requires the conscious use of skills, some of which may be learnt. But the most evocative and meaningful art has been 'channelled' from a deeper source, giving it a numinous/spiritual/meaningful quality and the ability to resonate with the viewer's depths. True artists tap into a source which conveys something deep to the audience. Theatre and film can at best feel as if the actor is channelling the character portrayed and conveying something beyond the actor's everyday personality. This can be deeply affecting. Think of the emotion music conveys. A painting which lacks this quality will likely leave the viewer cold and untouched.

Abstract Expressionist artist Mark Rothko (1903–70) may be a good example. His paintings are notoriously blank canvasses of basically one colour in many cases. There is a whole series of maroon paintings; another which are all black. It sounds dull doesn't it? And yet… when the author has sat in a gallery looking at his paintings 'in the flesh', they are deeply moving, conveying complex layers of feelings and emotions. How is this possible? I would suggest this is because of the deep link they convey to depths of human experience not encountered in the diurnal world even though they are accessible to those with an eye to 'see'.

Many artists are fascinated by the unconscious and indeed try to convey it. Alfred Hitchcock famously employed Salvador Dali (1904–89) to create a dream sequence in his film *Spellbound* (1945), which is a clunky attempt to convey something which it is almost impossible to communicate. The nature of both dreams and the unconscious can really only be experienced first hand.

ANIMALS

Finally, mention should be made of our connection to animals. It would not be strictly seen as belonging in the realm of the unconscious in the usual sense of the word, but falls within the realm of the mysterious, the telepathic (meaning distant feeling) and the uncanny. We have probably all experienced unexplainable phenomena with animals. How do they know when their owners are about to arrive home? How do they know when their owners are ill? It is well known that dogs can detect when their owners are ill and have saved lives by alerting the owner to seek medical attention; for example, the animal being drawn to a changed smell in an area where cancer has begun. Or when they detect an owner is about to have an epileptic fit. It is worth quoting Sheldrake who cites an impressive anecdote of such a case:

> [the dog] can sense, up to 50 minutes before, that I am going to
> have an attack and taps me twice with his paw, giving me time to get
> somewhere safe. He can also press a button on my phone and bark
> when it is answered, to get help, and, if he thinks I'm going to have an
> attack while I am in the bath, he'll pull the plug out.

(2011 p.196)

How do salmon 'return home' to their place of birth, or birds know where/how to migrate? Young birds even migrate to areas where they have never been before without being led by birds who 'know the way'. Many insects do the same. Jung sees extra-sensory perception as a manifestation of the collective unconscious which:

> behaves as if it were one and not as if it were split up into many individuals. It is non-personal ... It is the same everywhere and at all times ... As it is not limited to the person, it is also not limited to the body. It manifests itself therefore not only in human beings but also at the same time in animals and even in physical circumstances.
>
> (Jung, *Letters*, Vol. 1 dated November 1945, p.395)

Jung then cites the following:

> I walk with a woman patient in a wood. She tells me about the first dream in her life that had made an everlasting impression upon her. She had seen a spectral fox coming down the stairs in her parental home. At this moment a real fox comes out of the trees not 40 yards away and walks quietly on the path ahead of us for several minutes. The animal behaves as if it were a partner in the human situation. (One fact is no fact, but when you have seen many, you begin to sit up).
>
> (Jung, *Letters*, Vol. 1 dated November 1945, p.395)

Biologist Rupert Sheldrake has written directly about this topic (2011). This cannot be explained only by the dog's ability to hear or smell more acutely than us. Neither is it connected to regular routine or recognising the owner's car as this happens even when the owner comes home at random times, without a vehicle or in an unknown vehicle. Sheldrake researched in some detail and adopts a scientific approach. His book is filled with examples of the connection between owner and animal as well as of the healing potential of owning them. An example:

> Some people who suffer with migraines have dogs that come and lie with them while they are suffering. Frau R. Huber of Horgen, Switzerland, found that her dog Nero also knew on which side of her head she had the migraine. 'If it was the right side he excitedly and vigorously licked my right eye and my right forehead with a low

whimper. If the pain was on the left he did the same on the other side.
It was like a massage'.

(Sheldrake 2011 p.77)

Sheldrake sees these phenomena in terms of what he calls a morphic field, which he visualises as being like an elastic band connecting creatures and objects. See the discussion of what Jung called the *unus mundus* (one world) above.

Equine-assisted therapy is a method where therapists work with horses as co-therapists. Horses too have an uncanny ability to tune in to what is going on with humans and have been shown to have extraordinary powers to heal and help people who turn to them in times of need.

A final example from the animal world is the case of the Asian Tsunami in 2004. Many people noticed that animals were behaving in unusual ways. As well as being able to detect internal dangers (see above for a discussion of animals picking up an owner's illness), they are able to recognise imminent danger in the outside world. In an unpublished talk (2013), Antonia Boll (British Jungian analyst) cites the case of the Asian Tsunami when she tells the story of a colleague sailing in the Indian Ocean at the time of the Boxing Day Tsunami in 2004:

She and others in her group awoke to find the sea and sky an unusual colour of purple. Thinking nothing of it they took a small launch and headed for an island that turned out to be 50 nautical miles from the epicentre of the quake. As they were settling down to explore, they noticed it was impossible to place their mats on the beach. Everywhere they looked, hoards of ants were running in helter-skelter directions. Sensing the ants knew something they did not, [my colleague]'s group read their activity as a sign to move away from the beach as quickly as possible. The only way was uphill.

Fortunately they had the sense to take heed and follow the animals:

The ants had sensed danger in the earth's tremors and were moving away from the beach. [My colleague] had a lucky escape! At the time of the Tsunami, I also heard about groups of elephants who were seen heading for higher ground. The humans who followed their example and fled inland were saved from the devastating tidal waves that followed. Anthropologists expected the aboriginal population of the Andaman Islands to be wiped out but they heeded their folklore tradition which speaks of a "huge shaking of ground followed by a high wall of water". The Onge aboriginals all survived.

SUMMARY

In this chapter we have looked at the history of the discovery of the unconscious, and then looked at the personal, the collective (of which more appears in Chapter 3 on Archetypes) and the psychoid unconscious. We looked at the function, or purpose, of the unconscious, and then Jung's model of the unconscious. A review has been made of Jung's voluminous writings on the unconscious. This has included synchronicity. We have looked at how the unconscious can manifest in physical form by way of psychosomatic illness, for example including intergenerational trauma. And then we focused on manifestations in film and art. Finally, we have reviewed how animals and humans may be connected by an unconscious thread.

REFERENCES

Bernstein, J.S. (2005) *Living in the Borderland: The Evolution of Consciousness and the Challenge of Healing Trauma*. Hove: Routledge.

Bohm, D. (1980) *Wholeness and the Impicate Order*. Oxon & New York: Routledge Classics, 2002.

Boll, A. (2013) *Listening to the Earth's Tremors: The Helpful Animal as Catalyst in the Journey Towards Wholeness* (unpublished talk).

Cambray, J. (2009) *Synchronicity: Nature & Psyche in an Interconnected Universe*. College Station, TX: Texas A&M University Press.

Ellenberger, H.F. (1970) *The Discovery of the Unconscious: The History and Evolution of Dynamic Psychiatry*. New York: Basic Books.

von Franz, M-L. (1992) *Psyche and Matter*. Boston, MA: Shambhala.

Grand, S. & Salberg, J. (Eds.) (2017) *Trans-generational Trauma and the Other: Dialogues Across History and Difference*. London & New York: Routledge.

Hesse, H. (1972) *Steppenwolf*. London: Penguin.

Hitchcock, A. (Director) (1945) *Spellbound*. Selznick International Pictures.

James, W. (1982) *Varieties of Religious Experience*. London & New York: Penguin Classics, 1902.

Jung, C.G. (1939 [1958]) "Psychological Commentary on the Tibetan Book of the Great Liberation", in CW 11, 1969.

Jung, C.G. (1944) "The Conjunction" in CW14, 1963.

Jung, C.G. (1951) "On Synchronicity" in CW8, 1960.

Jung, C.G. (1952) "Synchronicity: An Acausal Connecting Principle" in CW8, 1960.

Jung, C.G. (1954) "On the Nature of the Psyche" in CW8, 1960.

Jung, C.G. (1958) "A Psychological View of Conscience" in CW10, 1964.

Jung, C.G. (1963) *Memories, Dreams, Reflections*. London: Fontana Press, 1995.

Jung, C.G. (1973) *C.G. Jung Letters. Vol. 1: 1906–1950* (Ed. G. Adler & A. Jaffé; Trans. R.F.C. Hull). London: Routledge & Kegan Paul.

Laszlo, E. (2004) *Science and the Akashic Field: An Integral Theory of Everything*. Rochester, VT: Inner Traditions. (2nd edition 2007.)

Main, R. (1997) *Jung on Synchronicity and the Paranormal*. Princeton, NJ: Princeton University Press.

Main, R. (2007) *Revelations of Chance: Synchronicity as Spiritual Experience*. New York: SUNY.

McDougall, J. (1989) *Theatres of the Body: A Psychoanalytical Approach to Psychosomatic Illness*. London: Free Association Books.

Russack, N. (2002) *Animal Guides: In Life, Myth and Dreams*. Toronto: Inner City Books.

Salberg, J. & Grand, S. (Eds.) (2017) *Wounds of History: Repair and Resilience in the Trans-generational Transmission of Trauma*. London & New York: Routledge.

Sheldrake, R. (2009) *Morphic Resonance: The Nature of Formative Causation*. Rochester, VT: Park Street Press.

Sheldrake, R. (2011) *Dogs that Know When Their Owners Are Coming Home: The Unexplained Powers of Animals*. London: Arrow Books.

Stone, M. (2006) "The Analyst's Body as Tuning Fork: Embodied Resonance in Countertransference" in *Journal of Analytical Psychology* Vol. 51. pp. 109–124.

Tarnas, R. (2006) *Cosmos and Psyche: Intimations of a New World View*. New York & London: Penguin Viking.

THE STRUCTURE OF THE PSYCHE

"Nobody can say where man ends."

(Jung 1957 p.301)

This chapter is concerned with what we might call the nuts and bolts of the psyche; how it is structured. We will look at (1) Jung's model of the psyche, (2) Edward Edinger's Ego/Self axis and (3) the place of soul and spirit. Then more briefly by way of comparison we turn to (4) Freud's models of the psyche, and finally (5) Post-Jungian models of the Self.

JUNG'S MODEL OF THE PSYCHE

> The basic structure of the Jungian psyche is made up of: ego, self, personal unconscious and collective unconscious. The ego uses a persona (or mask) as an interface to the outside world. The interface between the ego and the inner world is seen as the anima or animus. The archetypes (which make up the collective unconscious) are represented by mythological motifs, personified images (such as Clown, Sorcerer, Angel), symbolic events or symbolic transitions in life we all encounter. (For full discussion of archetypes see Chapter 3.) The self (sometimes spelt with a capital 'S' to emphasise its central place in the schema) is the ordering principle of the entire personality.

The unconscious has a chapter devoted to itself (Chapter 1). And anima and animus are discussed in Chapters 3 and 8. So here we will look at the other important structural elements of the psyche.

Ego, self and persona are terms Jung used to describe different facets of our psychological make-up. Jung saw the psyche as encompassing not merely the psychological dimension, but also the soul. In fact, the German word he uses for psyche is 'Seele', which means soul. Jung understands psyche as "the totality of all psychic processes, conscious as well as unconscious" (1971 p. 463).

Taking each of these elements in turn:

Ego. Jung characterises the ego as:

> stand[ing] to the self as the moved to the mover, or as object to subject, because the determining factors which radiate out from the self surround the ego on all sides and are therefore supraordinate to it. The self, like the unconscious, is an *a priori* existent out of which the ego evolves.
>
> (1954 par. 391)

The way 'ego' is used colloquially (meaning to be puffed up and inflated) needs to be put to one side for a moment as 'ego' is used in psychological parlance in a way which is both more nuanced and complex. We need to take account of three different aspects to it, namely:

(a) as the core of consciousness,
(b) as part of the structure of the psyche, especially in its relation to the self, and
(c) in terms of developmental stages over the course of a lifetime.

(Samuels 1986 p.56)

A strong and healthy ego enables us to function well in relation to the world. There are times – such as during mental illness, or vulnerability in the face of the vicissitudes of life – when the ego becomes less robust and therefore needs to be bolstered. This can happen with loving care, or making a success of things in other ways which help us feel good about ourselves. Life involves a constant rebalancing.

People who do not have a very developed ego can feel like a burden as they lean on others in the absence of any core psychological strength or sense of direction in themselves.

The dream ego is the overarching character/experience through whose eyes the dream is seen.

The ego is the conscious personality. It is developing from birth and continues to mature throughout life. The conscious elements of the psyche are channelled via the ego; so the ego manages everyday functions.

Persona is the term Jung adopted to describe the interface between the ego and the world. Persona was the name of the masks worn by actors in ancient antiquity. Even modern Greek and Japanese drama will at times use masks as a device to convey different characteristics or moods. Anecdotally, if you have ever worn a mask it can be a powerful, even uncanny, experience whereby you find yourself taking on the character of the mask. This is a technique sometimes used in experimental humanistic psychotherapy groups.

Taking on a different persona is something we have probably all done. People joke about having a 'telephone voice' or adopt an accent to blend in. Others are so invested in their careers that they think they 'are' lawyers, doctors, psychoanalysts or teachers. Parental roles can feel so entrenched that it is difficult to know who you are beyond that role, which is why parents can feel so bereft and suffer from empty nest syndrome when the children leave home. Who are you when your parenting is no longer required? These are personas we adopt. I do not mean to imply it is wrong to do so. It is important to take on these roles and to take responsibility for carrying out all these functions, but it must also be remembered that at the core that is not who we are in an existential sense.

Jung saw the dissolution of the persona in analysis (which is not to say elimination, which would not be possible or desirable) as opening the door to fantasy (1916 par. 470) in that collective pressure to conform is ameliorated. A persona can become too rigid, like a mask which obscures what lies underneath rather than acting as a vehicle to communicate the contents of the underlying mind, including feelings.

At a party, your persona will be of great value to you, enabling you to interact in a social context with more ease. In an intimate context, it could become a defence from greater closeness; something to hide behind.

Persona is not to be confused with the 'false self' posited by eminent English paediatrician and psychoanalyst Donald Winnicott (1896–1971) (discussed in Chapter 4), which is more about compliance and inauthenticity.

Self is seen as the central core of the psyche which has greater gravitas. While the ego is the centre of consciousness, the self is the subject of the whole psyche since it includes the unconscious. Jung states that:

> The self is not only the centre but also the whole circumference which embraces both conscious and unconscious; it is the centre of this totality, just as the ego is the centre of conscious mind itself.
>
> (1952 par. 44)

The self is an archetypal symbol – the central, organising symbol – and as such belongs in the collective unconscious along with all the archetypes.

Samuels *et al* describe the self as:

> An archetypal image of man's fullest potential and the unity of the personality as a whole. The self as a unifying principle within the human psyche occupies the central position of authority in relation to psychological life and, therefore, the destiny of the individual.
>
> (1986 p.135)

"Everything essential" Jung tells us, "happens in the self and the ego functions as a receiver, spectator, and transmitter" (1942 p.326).

At risk of creating ever deeper layers of complexity, it is important to say that there is both a personal and collective level to archetypes (of which the self is but one). An everyday version of the self, while being authentic and present and related, would contrast with what we might think of as a collective self (perhaps better designated with a capital 'S'), which might be closer to the spark of the infinite aspect of the self (discussed more fully below).

Elsewhere Jung explains:

> The self is by definition the totality of all psychic facts and contents. It consists of one side of our ego consciousness that is included in the unconsciousness like a smaller circle in a greater one. So the self is not only an unconscious fact, but also a conscious fact: the ego is the visibility of the self.... The self is a fact of nature and always appears as such in immediate experiences, in dreams and visions... it is the spirit in the stone, the great secret which has to be worked out, to be extracted from nature, because it is buried in nature herself.
>
> (1936 p.977)

The self encompasses darkness and light, black and white, psyche and soma (mind and body) and all opposites simultaneously as it is a symbol of wholeness.

In his autobiography (Jaffé 1963), Jung talks about having identified a No.1 and No.2 personality. The numbers are not intended to place them in a hierarchy. No.1 was linked to the daily life of the then schoolboy. Alongside this existence Jung tells us:

> There existed another realm, like a temple in which anyone who entered was transformed and suddenly overpowered by a vision of the whole cosmos, so that he could only marvel and admire... Here lived the "Other", who knew God as a hidden, personal, and at the same time supra-personal secret. Here nothing separated man from God.
>
> (Jaffé 1963 p.62)

The two personalities can be construed as relating to ego (No.1) and self (No.2). Mark Saban (contemporary Jungian analyst in the UK and Lecturer at the Department of Psychosocial & Psychoanalytic Studies, University of Essex) suggests that Jung needed both these aspects since:

> when he attempted to live exclusively in the realm of either No.1 or No.2, he did not flourish as a human being. To the extent that Jung eventually achieved a mature attitude toward this state of affairs, that attitude consisted in an acceptance of the interminable nature of the play and counterplay between the two personalities. For Jung, it became not a question of either/or, but rather of both/and.
>
> (2013 p.21)

Saban interestingly suggests that this dual aspect was lived out in Jung's decision to live simultaneously in two houses: Küsnacht and Bollingen (ibid.). Jung also connected this dual aspect to his mother's daytime and night-time personalities.

Finally, Jung saw mandalas as a symbol of the self. While mandalas are discussed in Chapter 4, it is worth quoting the following passage from Jung's autobiography, which shows how he developed this idea and the importance he placed on them:

> In 1918–19 I was in Château d'Oex as Commandant de la Région Anglaise des Internés de Guerre. While I was there I sketched every morning in a notebook a small circular drawing, a mandala, which seemed to correspond to my inner situation at the time. With the help

of these drawings I could observe my psychic transformations from
day to day... Only gradually did I discover what the mandala really
is: "Formulation, Transformation, Eternal Mind's eternal recreation"
[a quote from Faust pt.2]. And that is the self, the wholeness of the
personality... My mandalas were cryptograms concerning the state of
the self which were presented to me anew each day. In them I saw the
self – that is, my whole being – actively at work.

(Jaffé 1963 pp.220–21)

Picasso expresses a similar sentiment about his own art: "The work
that one does is a way of keeping a diary" (Tériade 1932 quoted in
Borchardt-Hume & Ireson 2018 p.44).

EGO/SELF AXIS

The relation of ego to self is discussed in depth in Edinger (1972).
The relationship is an evolving one over the course of a lifetime in
that, as a baby, the two are merged and it is the work of each of us to
assimilate the needs of both as we mature into adulthood. Edinger
has created a series of diagrams which illustrate the progression of
this development in a set of four images whereby initially the ego is
subsumed within the self (like a small circle within a larger circle); the
ego subsequently partly emerges out of the self but there is an area of
overlap which can be visualised as a Venn diagram. The third shows
the ego separating further so there is less overlap, and finally the ego
separates entirely from the self to such an extent that the self has
consciousness of the connection between the two. Edinger acknowledges this final state is probably not achievable in reality. He draws
a line in his diagram from the centre of one circle to the centre of
the other linking ego and self, which he designates the Ego/Self axis
referring to the connection between the two entities. These images
are used purely as a device to discuss such slippery ideas which are
difficult to grasp. The ego and self are not physical entities like kidneys
and livers, which we can accurately draw. Edinger acknowledges that
this schema in the diagrams is only accurate so far as the point he
is making. They do not represent a concrete reality, but rather he is
trying to illustrate a psychological process. The self is usually defined
in Jungian psychology as the totality of the psyche, which would
include the ego. Edinger calls the self a paradox.

The relationship between ego and self is of crucial importance in functioning in the world. They both have their place to play and need to be kept in appropriate balance. Too much ego would mean being rather shallow and empty; too much self might mean a person has difficulty functioning in the external world in a way that is conducive to good relationships. A person might become too ponderous. This is generally not a conscious decision but the psyche has a way of balancing itself homeostatically. Greater connection with the self may be achieved however by consciously working on matters at depth and attaining greater contact with it. By the same token, a stronger connection to ego may be achieved by attention to relationships with others and ameliorating anxieties and social phobias.

SOUL AND SPIRIT

Soul and spirit are aspects of the human make-up that are seen as transpersonal, which means they are beyond the personal sphere and yet we are all connected to these realms. Essentially the soul reaches down towards the earth, and the spirit up towards the sky, although they are aspects – poles – of the same energy with different affective characteristics. They are sometimes talked about in hushed, 'religious', tones. Both realms are often seen as disconnected from humans, as if they are separate entities. It can be easier to think about both these elements as if they were cut off from us because on the one hand we are seduced into inflation by their power, and on the other awed or spooked as if it is impossible for us to be connected to such sublime energies. And yet, as Ann Baring reminds us (quoted Chapter 7), "we – evolved from the very substance of the stars – can know that we participate in the mysterious ground of spirit while living in this physical dimension of reality" (2013 p. 458).

Jung sees soul as being the very essence of relationship (1946 p.293). He talks about it at length in terms of anima. The dream, for Jung, is a "hidden doorway in the innermost and most secret recesses of the soul, opening into that cosmic night which was psyche long before there was any ego-consciousness" (1934 par. 304).

We long to be connected to these realms when we feel separated from them. They are our deepest nature. There is a pertinent

Hebrew parable which speaks to this and goes as follows. We are born on the understanding that we 'forget' where we came from, ie the lap of G-d, which leaves us forever with a longing to return but not being able to locate the source of that yearning. The teaching is called the *Aggadic Midrash* based on a passage in *Talmud Masechet Nidah*:

> Before a child is born, a light is held behind its head, with which it can see from one end of the world to the other, and they teach it the whole of Torah. But at the moment of birth an angel touches it on the lips and it forgets all. So all of life is spent remembering what we once knew.
>
> (1977 p.367)

The story continues: "Therefore we all have a dent below our nose which is where the angel touched us" (with thanks to Rabbi David Freeman for the full quote and reference).

That idea might need some time to reflect on, to allow it to sink in, before we change mode to thinking about the next section which puts us in an altogether different mind space, perhaps of significance in itself in differentiating the vastly different modes of thinking between a Jungian and a Freudian approach, which tends to be more purely cerebral.

SUMMARY

We have looked at Jung's model of the psyche including the place of soul and spirit. The unconscious is covered in Chapter 1; anima/us in Chapters 3 and 8. So that here we discussed ego, persona and self followed by Edinger's formulation of the Ego/Self axis.

FREUD'S MODELS OF THE PSYCHE

The Freudian method was and is predominantly concerned with looking backwards to childhood and the roots or causes of problems, whereas Jung adopted a teleological approach which is concerned with the meaning and purpose of a symptom which may well involve looking backwards. By way of comparison, I will briefly lay out Freud's two models of the psyche as they evolved over his lifetime. In both cases repression is seen as being of central importance, which means that the unconscious represses insights, feelings or thoughts which are felt to be taboo or otherwise unwanted.

TOPOGRAPHICAL

Initially Freud thought of the psyche as a tripartite model, which was described as topographical. This refers to the shape of the pattern of the schema as he envisaged it. (Topography is a geographic term to describe the lay of the land.) The three components were seen as:

- Conscious,
- Unconscious and
- Preconscious mental processes

(Freud 1905 SE8 p.176 n1)

In the topographical model the mind is seen as in two portions – one repressed (unconscious) and the other repressing (conscious). The unconscious is seen as being opposed by the ego. Much of the ego is unconscious so that only part of it is covered by the term preconscious.

The topographical model was superseded by the structural model around 1923.

STRUCTURAL

The structural model, which remains in use to this day, is also tripartite, being made up of:

- Id
- Ego
- Superego

The 'Id' is seen as the instinctual aspect, actor of wild, unrestrained behaviour; the reservoir of libido (in the Freudian sense) and therefore referring to sexual acting out for example. It is not restrained by social conventions or conscience.

The ego encompasses the functions of censorship and reality-testing. It has two distinct definitions for Freud:

1. to distinguish a person as a whole (including the body) from others, and as
2. part of the mind. (This aspect has sometimes been translated as self.)

Superego is the home of conscience, guilt, remorse, punishment. It holds the function of prohibition. Freud moved from referring to ego-ideal to superego, which perhaps points to a striving towards perfection – so prevalent in society today – which can be demoralising in that it cannot be attained. Think of the pressure on young people to have plastic surgery or fake tans, or to be the 'right' weight/size/shape. These are all superego demands.

As with Jung's writings, Freud uses the same word in different contexts to mean something slightly different. For example 'unconscious' is seen variously to mean:

1. quality of experience
2. mental "system", and
3. the dynamic Unconscious.

These slippages into different usage of the same word do not imply that a mistake was made. Rather it is that these pioneering thinkers were developing their thought over extended periods and were able to acknowledge advances as they arose.

Freud's method of dream interpretation is discussed in Chapter 6.

DANIEL STERN (1934–2012)

As we move on to look at modern developments in thinking about the self, it is important to give even the briefest nod to the formulation of Daniel Stern, prominent American (non-Jungian) specialist in infant development, who conceived of the self as follows:

- sense of an emerging self
- sense of a core self
- sense of subjective self
- sense of verbal self.

(Jacoby 2006 p.32)

Stern's volume on child development (1985) is a classic in the field.

POST-JUNGIAN MODELS OF THE SELF

Contemporary Jungians have developed important new thinking about the nature of the self. The status of the concept as being so central in the psyche justifies allowing additional space to the subject. Although the following would not be a starting place in terms of learning about Jung, in the interests of pointing to directions for further study if you are minded to do so, it is worth briefly reviewing the most significant writers who have made contributions on the self:

1. **Michael Fordham** (1905–95) (co-editor of the English version of Jung's Collected Works based in the UK) developed a model beginning with the primary or original self which has no features. Fordham considered that individuation began in childhood. Fordham developed a model which involved what he called integration (stable), deintegration (unstable) and reintegration, which operate cyclically. Deintegration, although it sounds like disintegration, refers to a process of reaching for what needs to be incorporated, or differentiated as 'other'. It is quite difficult to understand!

Samuels *et al*, referring to Fordham and early infant development, summarise it as follows:

> [The] primary self contains all the innate, archetypal potentials that may be given expression by a person. In an appropriate environment, these potentials commence a process of *deintegration* emerging from the original unconscious integrate. They seek correspondences in the outer world. The resultant 'mating' of an active infant's archetypal potential and the mother's reactive responses is then *reintegrated* to become an internalised object. The deintegrative/reintegrative process continues throughout life.
>
> (1986 p.136)

Urban summarises Fordham's position:

> The model as it stood in its most mature form drew upon several concepts: the primary self, deintegration, reintegration, self-objects, self representations, and individuation.... Fordham's starting point is before and beyond all phenomena, and hence refers to a phenomenon-less state... that is 'empty' of phenomena, so that it is 'nothing but' potential.
>
> (2005 p.575; see also *Explorations into the Self* – Fordham 1985)

2. **Edward Edinger** (1922–98)

It is worth quoting Edinger (eminent American psychiatrist and Jungian analyst) at some length:

> The Self is the ordering and unifying centre of the total psyche (conscious and unconscious) just as the ego is the centre of the conscious personality. Or... the ego is the seat of the subjective identity while the Self is the seat of objective identity. The Self is thus the supreme psychic authority and subordinates the ego to it. The Self is most simply described as the inner empirical deity and is identical with the imago Dei. Jung has demonstrated that the Self has a characteristic phenomenology. It is expressed by certain typical symbolic images called mandalas.
>
> (1972 pp.3–4)

The phenomenon of mandalas is discussed in Chapter 4 on Individuation. Edinger sets out a range of associated themes and images which he links to the Self:

> wholeness, totality, the union of opposites, the central generative point, the world navel, the axis of the universe, the creative point where God and man meet, the point where transpersonal energies flow into personal life, eternity as opposed to the temporal flux, incorruptibility, the inorganic united paradoxically with the organic, protective structures capable of bringing order out of chaos, the transformation of energy, the elixir of life – all refer to the Self, the central source of life energy, the fountain of our being which is most simply described as God.
>
> (1972 p.4)

It is important to use the 'G' word sparingly as it can be alienating to some. Jung himself speaks to this when he says:

> [T]he term *self* is often mixed up with the idea of God. I would not do that. I would say that the term *self* should be reserved for that sphere which is within the reach of human experience, and we should be very careful not to use the word God too often. As we use it, it borders on impertinence... The experience of the self is so marvellous and so complete that one is of course tempted to use the conception of God to express it.... we should reserve that term God for a remote deity that is supposed to be the absolute unity of all singularities. The self would be the preceding stage, a being that is more than man... that is the thinker of our thoughts, the doer of our deeds, the maker of our lives, yet is still within the reach of human experience.
>
> (1936 pp.977–8)

Jung being Jung, he elsewhere uses the term himself: "[the self] might equally well be called 'the God within us'" (1945 par. 399). A frequent difficulty with Jung is that he does at times contradict himself! In his autobiography he puts it succinctly: "I am [meaning we all are – RW] a splinter of the infinite deity" (Jaffé 1963 p.17).

3. **Erich Neumann** (1905–60), one of the first-generation Jungian analysts and Jung's friend from the 1930s, was considered to be the foremost practitioner in Israel although he was theoretically something of an outsider and an early adopter of many psycho-analytic concepts, albeit that he made them his own. His work is rarely referenced in a clinical context but his writing is of import-ance. He roots the early development of self in the baby's relation to the mother whom he sees:

> as carrying the image of the baby's self in unconscious projection or even functioning 'as' the baby's self. Since in infancy the child cannot experience the characteristics of an adult self, the mother reflects or acts as a 'mirror'.... The first conscious experiences of the self derive from perceptions of her and interactions with her.... The baby's gradual separation from his mother may be compared with the ego's emergence from the self and the image he develops of his relationship to his mother forms the basis of his subsequent attitude toward the self and the unconscious in general.
>
> (Samuels *et al.* 1986 p.137)

Jacoby tells us that this idea was not universally accepted. Jolande Jacobi (1890–1973), early Jungian analyst and contemporary of Jung: "attacked the idea of the mother as Self. She was convinced that the Self was a metaphysical reality that comes into contact with human experience" (Jacoby 2006 p.27).

For Neumann, "the first phase of child development is dominated by the instinct of self-preservation and the drive to self-development" (1973 p.28). He goes on:

> The unfolding of the relations between ego and thou between ego and body, and between ego and Self, which in the primal relationship are inextricably bound together, is among the essential processes of child development... From the very outset, not only the development of the ego, but the over-all viability of the individual depend on the nature of the relations between ego and Self.
>
> (1973 p.44)

Neumann takes Edinger's Ego/Self axis a step further and contends that, in the second half of life, the ego and Self move back together again (referring to Edinger's diagram described above) (1973 p.47).

4. **Edward Whitmont** (1912–88) is from the Classical School of Analytical Psychology, steeped in mythology and symbolic thought. Together with Sylvia Brinton Perera he has written one of the best books on dreams in analysis (1989). For him the symbolism of the self:

> expressing as it does an unknown superordinated, directive and encompassing entity, tends to appear in the form of mythologems... The *modus operandi* of the Self may be likened to the centre of an energy field which aims toward fulfilling a life and personality pattern which as a potentiality is *a priori* given"

(1969 p.219)

5. **Warren Colman** (contemporary Jungian analyst in London) in his 2008 paper distinguishes the difference between being conscious ('core consciousness') and knowing that one is conscious (self-reflexive consciousness) before differentiating between three different aspects of the self:

   a) the overall process of psychosomatic *being* which we share with all living creatures and which expresses itself through action (self as totality),
   b) the conscious awareness of *knowing* the self that is a peculiarly human phenomenon consequent on the development of symbolic imagination (sense of self including numinous experiences of self), and
   c) *having* a self (or soul) as an essential attribute of being human that can only be achieved through being endowed with a self in the mind of others.

(2008 p.351)

6. **Louis Zinkin** (1926–93) (Jungian analyst based in London) presents a constructivist view of the self. He considers some of the paradoxes in Jungian definitions and compares these to Winnicott. He proposes we think in terms of people in social interaction with each other rather than as solitary subjects as Jung did (2008 p.389). For Zinkin:

The self comes into existence only through interaction with others
and the form it takes, the sense the individual has of being or having
a self, will depend greatly on the culture in which he or she has been
brought up.

(ibid. p.394)

This leads us neatly on to the final section in this chapter.

NO-SELF

To bring this section on the self to a close I want – perhaps paradoxically –
to touch on the Buddhist notion of 'no-self' as set out by Jungian analyst and practising Buddhist, Polly Young-Eisendrath in the US:

The no-self approach... embraces nothing like a blueprint of a true self.
In place of such a teleology is a focus on mutual discovery within a safe
therapeutic environment... the patient and therapist inevitably collide
with... relational dilemmas in which they can observe how the self is
disrupted and re-established... [T]hey open up profound appreciation
for interdependence and a confidence rooted in something other than
ego. These therapeutic skills include mindful awareness of subjectivity
and intersubjectivity, a deep belief in mutual discovery

(2009 pp.92–3)

From the archetype of the 'self', we now move on to looking at the
theory of archetypes and focus on a number of other examples.

SUMMARY

We have looked at Jung's model of the psyche, including the place of
soul and spirit, and Edinger's Ego/Self axis, before contrasting this
with Freud's models of the psyche (both topographical and structural). We then looked at a range of post-Jungian models of the Self
including a Buddhist approach to no-self.

REFERENCES

Assembly of Rabbis of the Reform Synagogues of Great Britain (Eds) (1977)
Forms of Prayer for Jewish Worship (7th edition). London: The Reform
Synagogues of Great Britain.

Baring, A. (2013) *The Dream of the Cosmos: A Quest for the Soul*. Dorset: Archive Publishing.

Borchardt-Hume, W. & Ireson, N. (2018) Picasso 1932: Love Fame Tragedy. London: Tate Publishing.

Colman, W. (2008) "On Being, Knowing and Having a Self" in *Journal of Analytical Psychology* Vol. 53 No. 3. pp. 351–366.

Edinger, E.F. (1972) *Ego and Archetype: Individuation and the Religious Function of the Psyche*. New York: G.P. Putnam's Sons.

Fordham, M. (1985) *Explorations into the Self*. London: Karnac Books, 2001.

Freud, S. (1905) *The Complete Psychological Works of Sigmund Freud. Vol. VIII* (referred to as the Standard Edition or "SE"). London: Hogarth Press, 1961.

Jacoby, M. (2006) "Neumann's Concept of the Primary Relationship in the Light of Contemporary Infant Research" in *Harvest* Vol. 52 No. 2. pp. 26–35.

Jaffé, A. (1963) Memories, Dreams, Reflections. London: Fontana Press, 1995.

Jung, C.G. (1916) "Structure of the Unconsious" in CW7.

Jung, C.G. (1934) "The Meaning of Psychology for Modern Man" in CW10.

Jung, C.G. (1936) *Nietzsche's Zarathustra: Notes on the Seminar given in 1934–1939 by C.G. Jung*. (Ed. J.L. Jarrett). Volume 2. London: Routledge, 1989.

Jung, C.G. (1942) "Letter to Aniela Jaffé 22nd December 1942" in *C.G. Jung Letters. Vol. 1: 1906–1950*. (Ed. G. Adler & A. Jaffé; Trans. R.F.C. Hull). London: Routledge & Kegan Paul.

Jung, C.G. (1945) "The Mana-Personality" in CW7.

Jung, C.G. (1946) *The Practice of Psychotherapy*, in CW16.

Jung, C.G. (1952) *Psychology and Alchemy*, in CW12.

Jung, C.G. (1954) "Transformation Symbolism in the Mass" in CW11.

Jung, C.G. (1955–56) *Mysterium Coniunctionis*, in CW14.

Jung, C.G. (1957) "The Houston Films" in *C.G. Jung Speaking: Interviews and Encounters* (Ed. W. McGuire & R.F.C. Hull). Princeton, NJ: Princeton University Press, 1977. pp. 276–352.

Jung, C.G. (1971) "Definitions" in *Psychological Types, CW6*.

Neumann, E. (1955) *The Great Mother*. London: Routledge & Kegan Paul.

Neumann, E. (1973) *The Child: Structure and Dynamics of the Nascent Personality*. London & New York: Routledge.

Saban, M. (2013) "Ambiguating Jung" in *How and Why We Still Read Jung: Personal and Professional Reflections* (Ed. J. Kirsch & M. Stein). London & New York: Routledge. pp. 35–65.

Samuels, A., Shorter, B. & Plaut, F. (1986) *A Critical Dictionary of Jungian Analysis*. London & New York: Routledge, 1997.

Stern, D. (1985) *The Interpersonal World of the Infant: A View from Psychoanalysis and Developmental Psychology*. New York: Basic Books.

Whitmont, E. (1969) *The Symbolic Quest: Basic Concepts in Analytical Psychology*. Princeton, NJ: Princeton University Press, 1991.

Whitmont, E. & Brinton Perera, S. (1989) *Dreams, a Portal to the Source*. Hove & New York: Routledge.

Young-Eisendrath, P. (2009) "Empty Rowboats: No-Blame and Other Therapeutic Effects of No-Self in Long-Term Psychotherapy and Psychoanalysis" in *Self and No-Self: Continuing the Dialogue Between Buddhism and Psychotherapy* (Ed. D. Mathers, M.E. Miller & O. Ando). London & New York: Routledge. pp.92–99.

Zinkin (2008) "Your Self: Did You Find It or Did You Make It?" in *Journal of Analytical Psychology* Vol.53 No.3. pp.389–406.

ARCHETYPES

I will begin by setting out the Jungian definition of archetype. Then I will lightly touch on a few examples with which you will be familiar (although you may not have thought of them in this way), before including some archetypal themes which may not be so immediately obvious, such as number, slavery, love, war, home, sacrifice and meaning.

DEFINITION

Archetype is a precise, technical term in Jungian speech which Jung first coined in 1919 in "Instinct and the Unconscious" (CW8 par. 270). Originally Jung had used the term 'primordial image' until he recognised that the manifestations of universal motifs were not limited to images but also arose as ideas, feelings, experiences and characteristic patterns of behaviour (Stevens 2006 p.76).

Archetypes are not to be confused with stereotypes. In everyday speech, the meanings are sometimes conflated. A stereotype is used to describe a hackneyed, trite or oversimplified idea/person.

ARCHETYPES CAN BE CONSTRUED AS:

- significant events (such as birth, death, falling in love, marriage, war)
- characters (Mother, Father, Hero, Wise Old Man/Woman etc)
- symbols (heart, crucifix, mandalas), and
- motifs (adolescence, midlife crisis, heartbreak, abandonment, transcendence)

Archetypes are not simply intellectual concepts but are imbued with feeling, which gives them their power to affect us in a most visceral fashion. You know when you are gripped by an archetype, such as falling in love. Or when you are possessed by the 'witch'; or the 'hero'. They have characteristics with which we may be familiar and encountering them in their archetypal form increases their impact significantly because archetypes are numinous (which means they are possessed of a spiritual quality/energy which increases their force and may be felt as overwhelming).

The word 'archetype' comes from two Greek words which translate as 'first pattern' or prototype. The term as Jung initially envisaged it can be construed as conveying something like a template which then becomes fleshed out with personal/cultural/historical data, creating a more specific/refined image or form. 'Mother' is an archetype but our respective cultures will fill this image with greater levels of complexity and nuance, and our personal mothers will create a more specific image of what being a mother means to each of us. Jung:

> Like any other archetype, the mother archetype appears under an almost infinite variety of aspects. I mention here only some of the more characteristic. First in importance are the personal mother and grandmother, stepmother and mother-in-law; then any woman with whom a relationship exists – for example a nurse or governess or perhaps a remote ancestress. Then there are what might be termed mothers in a figurative sense. To this category belongs the goddess, and especially the Mother of God, the Virgin, and Sophia. Mythology offers many variations on the mother archetype
>
> (1954a par. 156)

THEORETICAL ROOTS AND PHILOSOPHICAL INFLUENCES

The concept of archetypes can be found in Jung's earliest writings (1902) and culminates in Volume 9 of the Collected Works, which is divided into two parts. The first contains essays written from 1933 onwards, which sets out the theoretical basis of Jung's ideas. It then goes on to discuss certain archetypes in greater depth, which he links to the process of individuation (see Chapter 4). The second part of Volume 9 (entitled *Aion*) concerns the symbolism of the Self (seen as an archetype; covered in Chapter 2) on which Jung places great emphasis and therefore warrants an entire volume to itself.

An important distinction needs to be made between the archetypal image and the archetype-*an-sich* (itself) as it is called (following German philosopher Emmanuel Kant [1724–1804] who spoke of a 'Ding-an-sich' or thing in itself, meaning we are talking about the essence of something). The archetype-an-sich is the nature of the archetype, the structure or like the DNA; the image is how we visualise the archetype in the mind's eye. An archetype is a potential; it is the predisposition that is inherited, not the experience or quality itself. Jung clarifies his meaning when he emphasises that the term archetype:

> is not meant to denote an inherited idea, but rather an inherited mode of psychic functioning, corresponding to the inborn way in which the chick emerges from the egg, the bird builds a nest, a certain kind of wasp stings the motor ganglion of the caterpillar, and eels find their way to the Bermudas. In other words, it is a 'pattern of behaviour'.
>
> (1949a par. 1228)

The concept of an archetypal structure bears some resemblance to Plato's concept of universal ideas whereby 'ideas' "were pure mental forms originating in the minds of the gods before human life began, and as a consequence, they were supraordinate to the objective world of phenomena" (Stevens 2006 p.79).

Arthur Schopenhauer (German philosopher 1788–1860) was on to similar ideas when he spoke of 'prototypes', which he saw as the original forms of all things. Jung was influenced by these ideas.

Samuels *et al* remind us that archetypes:

are recognisable in outer behaviours, especially those that cluster around the basic and universal experiences of life such as birth, marriage, motherhood, death and separation. They also adhere to the structure of the human psyche itself and are observable in relation to inner or psychic life, revealing themselves by way of such inner figures as Anima, Shadow, Persona and so forth. Theoretically there could be any number of archetypes.

(1986 p.26)

The symbolic representation of what is signified in an archetypal image is absolutely precise and cannot be replaced by anything else. The archetype is fundamentally economic in its use of energy and the way it conveys its 'message' and meaning. An example would be a dream image of a person or thing which contains multiple layers of nuance but which the dreamer immediately recognises as pointing towards something they personally understand. We will often talk about a dream by saying "it was my brother, although it didn't look like him". We know the image refers to the 'brother' because of all the subtle, multiple layers condensed in the image.

Jung sees the archetypes as possessing both what he somewhat obscurely describes as ultra-violet and infra-red poles whereby the instinctual end is seen as being infra-red (implying blood red, full-bodied – including physiological reactions to situations such as a fast-beating pulse when in contact with an archetypal situation), and the spiritual aspect as being ultra-violet (Jung 1954b par. 414) (or shading towards blue, thus pointing to the sky and the spiritual dimension). An example would be the image of someone we find sexually alluring, a feeling which is experienced in a bodily way (the infra-red pole), and with whom there is a special connection that feels unique and 'meant', which has a spiritual quality to it (the ultra-violent pole). Both are contained within the same image; two sides of one coin.

COLLECTIVE UNCONSCIOUS

Jung's model of the psyche consists of the personal unconscious and the collective unconscious (see Chapter 1). Archetypes are conceptualised as being situated within the collective unconscious. They are not something which belongs on the personal/individual level; they are universal motifs. Myths and fairy tales are seen as an expression of the collective unconscious. They often have alternate versions in different cultures and at different points in time but with the same story or parables at their core. There are stories that are reimagined in modern form, such as *Bridget Jones' Diary* (Fielding 1996), which is a modern take on *Pride & Prejudice* (Austen [1813] 1996), or the film *Frozen* (Dir: Buck & Lee 2013), which is a modern take on *The Snow Queen* (Christian Anderson 2015). These are conscious reimaginings of the stories. But other stories appear in cultures or across time seemingly without any conscious link.

The Greek gods for example all have their equivalents in ancient Rome, although it may of course be that the Romans adopted Greek mythology in a conscious way and made them their own.

Greek god	Roman god
Zeus	Jupiter
Poseidon	Neptune
Hades	Pluto
Hera	Juno
Demeter	Ceres
Hestia	Vesta
Ares	Mars
Aphrodite	Venus

Jung saw the collective unconscious as being:

made up of contents which are formed personally only to a minor degree ... are essentially the same everywhere, and do not vary from man to man. This unconscious is like the air, which is the same everywhere, is breathed by everybody, and yet belongs to no one. Its contents (called archetypes) are the prior conditions or patterns of psychic formation in general. They have a... [potential and active existence...], ... They are in themselves non-perceptible, irrepresentable (since they precede all representation), everywhere and "eternally" the same. Hence there is only one collective unconscious, which is everywhere identical with itself, from which everything psychic takes shape before it is personalized, modified, assimilated, etc. by external influences.

(Jung 1973 Letters Vol. 1 to Pastor Max Frischknecht dated 8 February 1946, p.408)

Marie-Louise von Franz (1915–98) (Jung's contemporary and collaborator) sees the collective unconscious as "*the* living creative matrix of all our unconscious and conscious functionings, the essential structural basis of all our psychic life" (1974, p.4; emphasis in original).

Jung describes the archetypes variously as instinct (1956 par. 550), irrepresentable (1948 par. 223), innate (1954b par. 398) and bipolar in nature (1944 par. 553) by which he means they have opposite aspects which belong together; they are linked. This refers to Jung's formulation of the enantiodromia (a term taken from the pre-Socratic Greek philospher Heraclitus), meaning the tendency of things to change into their opposite. Like the pendulum, when things reach their limit, they swing back in the other direction and connect with their opposite so that the two extremes are linked along a continuum. Jung saw life as a continual balancing of opposites (1949b par. 1417). This can be a useful idea to hold in mind at times of trouble. Things do change. An example might be the way Professor Snape in *Harry Potter* starts as his nemesis and ends as his saviour (Rowling 2014).

SUMMARY

We have looked at the definition and theoretical roots of archetypes, differentiating archetype from stereotype. Then we have differentiated 'archetype' from 'archetype-an-sich'. Archetypes are situated within the collective unconscious.

IMAGES

Archetypes manifest in the form of inner imagoes or images:

King/Queen, Mother/Father, Child, Fairy, Witch
Saint, Dogsbody, Healer, Doctor/Nurse and Thief
Ghost, Murderer, Fool and Clown

These words all immediately evoke a cluster of images. Although they have different cultural and historical variants, we know what those words signify as we have encountered them. Volumes have been written on all of them so I have picked out just a few to illustrate the ideas.

The archetypes can be imagined as sub-personalities. Jung has personified them. The intention is not to imply there is a split personality in a pathological sense, but Jung used these images/figures to illustrate his thinking; to make complicated ideas digestible. It enables us to talk about such complex matters. Archetypal images provide a metaphor.

A few examples are given of a number of archetypes and how they might be recognised:

Anima/us: Jung's conception of anima and animus (the Latin word he used for the feminine and masculine versions of 'soul') is rather problematic. I will here set out an overview of Jung's use of this term, and then deal with the problems in Chapter 8. Jung describes the anima as "a factor of the utmost importance in the psychology of a man wherever emotions and affects are at work" (1954c par. 144). (You might begin to see the problems!) He sees the anima as being the feminine component that resides within all men, with women possessing an animus which is the counterpart representing the male component found in women. Jung:

> Every man carries within him the eternal image of a woman, not the image of this or that particular woman, but a definite feminine image. This image is fundamentally unconscious... an "archetype" of all the ancestral experiences of the female... Even if no woman existed, it would still be possible... to deduce... exactly how a woman would have to be constituted psychically. The same is true of the woman: she too has her inborn image of man.... Since this image is unconscious, it is... projected upon the person of the beloved, and is one of the chief reasons for passionate attraction or aversion.
>
> (1931 par. 338)

This is the seed of a useful idea although it has become both somewhat idealised and simplified, so these days you will hear reference to a man's 'feminine side'. Exploring the contrasexual aspect is something explored widely in culture. Think of Beyoncé's "If I Were a Boy" (2008) in which she explores what it is like to be male. Or

Virginia Woolf's *Orlando* (2016 [1928]), which was made into an award-winning film with Tilda Swinton (Dir: Potter 1993). Many contemporary Jungian thinkers now see all genders as possessing the whole range of possibilities so you will at times find writers referring to the anima's animus. The term is often used in dream analysis where a feminine figure is seen as representing an important aspect of a man's psyche; likewise for a male figure appearing in a woman's dreams. Most often the anima is seen as an ethereal creature while the animus is seen in rather more negative terms. There are countless examples of anima figures in literature and film. Think of Alicia Silverstone in *Clueless* (Dir: Heckerling 1995); Ingrid Bergman in *Casablanca* (Dir: Curtiz 1942); Cathy in *Wuthering Heights* (E. Bronte 1995 [1847]); pop singer Kate Bush particularly in her rendering of "Wuthering Heights", her debut single in 1978; Shakespeare's *Romeo and Juliet*, or any film with Marilyn Monroe. If you think of a luminous figure, you are probably dealing with the anima.

Mother/Father/Child are all archetypes. They barely require elaboration as we all know what those terms mean. We have all been at least one. In the case of the mother archetype, Marie-Louise von Franz breaks down the term: "With the archetype of the Great Mother you have the witch, the devilish mother, the beautiful wise old woman, and the goddess who represents fertility" (von Franz 1995 p.34). There are numerous facets to the archetype of the mother.

In describing the archetype of the father (like others such as mother and anima), it is important to take account of the political backdrop. A 1950s' father might be described as being the breadwinner who holds the boundaries at home and is the strong, authoritative influence. Nowadays when there is far greater equal distribution of tasks in the home, these have become stereotypical divisions. A way to think about this would be that the father archetype carries the template of boundary holding and authority etc, but that these tasks might be carried out by someone of any gender.

The archetype of the child metaphorically suggests the possibilities of new beginnings. The 'child' points us to the protective feelings elicited at the sight of an unspoiled creature who has yet to experience the challenges of life. The child, like an animal cub, is dependant and cannot meet its own needs. When we see children in crisis-hit areas having to cope without the support of an adult carer, our hearts break. Childhood is a phase that must be traversed. To remain stuck in the 'child' stage is a problem. Think of Peter Pan who remains a child eternally (Barrie 1980 [1911]).

What Jung means by **Shadow** is an agglomeration of all the characteristics with which we do not wish to be associated: "the thing he has no wish to be" (Jung 1946 par. 470). The archetype of the witch comes under the rubric of what Jung called the *Shadow*, as well as being an aspect of the mother archetype. (I have amplified the archetype of the witch elsewhere; Williams 2017). Coming to terms with the Shadow is a key necessity in both life and analysis. It enables one to take responsibility for one's faults and to withdraw blame. Those words however do not convey the power or the difficulty of encountering such an aspect of oneself. At the mild end it means realising there are aspects of oneself that need attention; feeling uncomfortable with a behaviour or attitude. But there are times when encountering the Shadow is a profoundly frightening experience and the visceral impact can be shattering. This is no mean feat; not for the faint-hearted. My account of the witch (2017) includes a series of dreams of 'the witch' which were terrifying. But by sticking with it, I gained enormous self-knowledge and a profoundly new attitude to life together with the confidence that I could cope with even such challenging aspects of life. These aspects need to be incorporated into a person as a whole. We all possess distasteful characteristics. That's just a fact of life.

There is a personal and collective level to archetypes. To give an example: A slip whereby you disparage someone 'accidentally' would be seen as a shadow aspect of the personal unconscious. The devil is a collective symbol which reflects the power, the numinosity, the awe associated with such an image. The collective aspect carries greater force. Jung encapsulates the difference: "it is quite within the bounds of possibility for a man to recognize the relative evil of his nature, but it is a rare and shattering experience for him to gaze into the face of absolute evil" (1951 par. 19).

- The **'Hero'** is superficially a much easier archetype with which to be identified although it does entail owning what to some people would be painful characteristics. Not everyone is comfortable being heroic (and I am including all genders within that category).

Every film has a hero at its centre and they are usually portrayed as being strong, positive and powerful; usually handsome too. The Hero gets the girl. What's not to like? Shy people would find such a presentation difficult to sustain; those who struggle with self-belief, introverts. Many people shun the limelight, while others thrive on it. Actors clamour for such parts. James Bond is a stereo-typical hero. Two complex examples come to mind who embody heroic characteristics but who produce ambivalent feelings. The first is *Dexter* (Dir: Dahl *et al* 2006–13), the story of a blood-spatter analyst in the Miami Metro Police Department working on murder cases and who is also a serial killer. He evokes great empathy and love, at the same time as revulsion at what he does. The second is Walter White in *Breaking Bad* (Dir: MacLaren *et al* 2008–13) who becomes a drug lord but whom you find yourself cheering and, again, feeling great empathy with.

- The **Trickster** is an archetypal character who is not straightfor-ward at all. Symbolically associated with Hermes, he is mercurial and slippery; looks deceive. S/he (albeit usually male) is cunning and defies authority; quick-thinking and capable of transforming situations in a flash. Think of Ali G (the satirical character created by Sacha Baron Cohen) or possibly certain politicians spring to mind. Think of Puck in Shakespeare's *Midsummer Night's Dream*. Or Bart Simpson. He is always engaged in some slippery under-taking and often fools and charms us with his quick wit.
- **Laughter** itself can be seen as an archetype. Humour is of course notoriously individual although some things are found amusing in all cultures (such as bodily functions). Types of humour aside, laughter itself is a universal experience, like happiness, sadness, play, love, hate. We all love to laugh. It is catching, even if there is no mutual language. It makes us feel good and connected to others. It might also be the case that, if one's environment does not provide the conditions for laughter to emerge, there is something wrong: a tension, something stifling one's potential or freedom to express oneself fully.
- **Number** is seen as an archetype. Although there are various systems of numbers such as Arabic (1, 2, 3) and Roman (I, II, III), the idea of numbers is an archetypal one with variants over time and place. Jung was working on numbers as he approached

the end of his life and, realising he would not complete the work, he handed his notes to his collaborator, Marie-Louise von Franz, who published her findings on number and time based on their joint research (1974). Jung had a hunch that natural numbers might be connected to what he called the *unus mundus* (one world in which everything is interconnected) by way of its relation to synchronicity. In 1928 sinologist (specialist in matters Chinese) Richard Wilhelm sent Jung a copy of *The Secret of the Golden Flower: A Chinese Book of Life* (1942) (a Chinese alchemical text to which Jung later added a European commentary). The timing was highly significant for Jung who was working on the early stages of studying medieval alchemy at the time, so Jung saw this coincidence as meaningful; a synchronicity. This led Jung to the study of the *I Ching* (Wilhelm [trans] 1951), which could be called an oracle and dates back to mythical antiquity. This is because the method on which the *I Ching* is based relies on synchronicity. (It is akin to using Tarot cards which are randomly drawn. With the *I Ching* the person consulting it throws coins or yarrow stalks which point the person to a particular passage which can be used as a guide.) Both branches of Chinese philosophy/religion – Confucianism and Taoism – take their inspiration from the *I Ching*. The *I Ching* is comprised of a highly mathematical schema of diagrams based on numbers which inspired Jung.

Von Franz cites examples of how mathematical systems had come into the consciousness of various mathematicians in a flash of synchronistic insight (1974 p.22). She refers to mathematician John Kreittner:

> [he] was deeply impressed by the amazing practical mathematical knowledge of the Sumerians and Babylonians and postulated that a kind of "instinctual mathematics" must exist in man which consists of a "direct perception of the relation between numbers".
>
> (ibid. p.27)

• **Slavery.** In Fanny Brewster's seminal work (2017) she talks of slavery being an archetypal event:

> People have enslaved each other for a very long time in one way or another. I believe that slavery is an archetypal event because the

form of slavery does exist in our psyches. We can see this in modern times as more children and women and sometimes men are taken into modern-day slavery. The words *human bondage* now more often make us think of individuals taken as sex slaves.

(2017 p.67)

She links this to archetypal grief in the following vignette:

My patient sits with me crying in a way that seems beyond any human suffering. I cannot comfort her. She is beyond my reach of nurturance-giving. I deeply feel her pain and anguish. I have known her sorrow. I understand that she isn't crying because of the death of her biological mother, who does still live.

Hers is the archetypal, intergenerational mourning for the passing of all failed mother-nurturance. This inevitable failure has occurred not because of anything my patient has done wrong, nor her mother before her. It is rather a result of the horrible success of slavery.

(ibid.)

The concept of slavery in its myriad forms preoccupy us on many levels (given their archetypal nature) and become fetishised in sexual play. Sub/dom (that is subordination and domination) themes are sometimes called sexual fetish but are actually within the realm of 'normal' sexuality. There is a vast sub-culture where people play with images of being dominated and enslaved in the world of sado-masochism (S&M). Or perhaps better to say it is in the culture as a whole. Samuels suggests that this theme reaches right back to the first couple. He recounts the Midrashic story (that is the ancient commentary on Hebrew scriptures):

[b]efore Eve was created there was Lilith. God created Adam and Lilith from the same dust. And on their first night in the garden, Adam mounts her to have sex with her. Then she says 'Get off me. Why should you lie on top of me in the superior position when we were made at the same time, from the same stuff?' He rapes her.

(1998 p.41)

Samuels draws our attention to the way in which the sub/dom politics of marital rape are hidden behind the seduction scene of Adam and Eve in the Garden of Eden, which is the usual, bowdlerised or idealised story that is more often told. Lilith is wiped out of the picture; her story is more rarely told, is kept in the shadows as something shameful which needs to be hidden.

- **Freedom** – the opposite of slavery – is an archetypal idea. Is that not what we all seek in one form or another? Not only personally, but collectively. There have been uprisings of people seeking freedom in every culture. The feeling of freedom is uplifting and numinous. Perhaps akin to...

- **Love** is an archetypal experience. Analysts often talk about sexuality and hate and sometimes what are crudely called 'perversions', but not so much about love. Love of course comes in many forms: mother-love, brotherly *phylia*, fellow feeling with friends, passion with a lover, commitment in a marriage. For some, love of God; love of one's vocation or career. Love of a sport even. These experiences all form part of individuation (see Chapter 4). In some languages there are many words for love to differentiate the particular form. Ancient Greek distinguishes as follows:

  - Agape denotes the highest form of unconditional love associated with charity and love of God as well as God's love of man.
  - Eros relates to passionate/sexual love; the realm of intimate relationships.
  - Phylia is used for affection as between equals.
  - Storge is another variant on affectionate fellow-feeling most often used as between parents and their children.

  Platonic love relates to a deep bond between partners but without sexual intimacy or desire.

  Love is an essential component of a fulfilled existence. Without it life becomes meaningless and empty. Its archetypal nature means we are deeply preoccupied with love (although not necessarily in a conscious way). Most films have love at their centre. We all want to be in love and need to be loved. It is a fundamental, existential or archetypal need. A spiritual or religious perspective might think that love is our essence as human beings.

- **Home** is an archetype we all experience daily. We generally feel safe at home. (If not, there is a problem.) People long to be home, both literally and metaphorically. We yearn for a physical home to hang a hat, a professional home among like-minded folk, to set up home with a loved-one. Homer's Odyssey (1946) is a paean to home as he journeys back from the Trojan Wars.

- **Sacrifice** is a noble archetype we all usually admire. It can take the form of religious adherence, mother's love or a soldier on the battlefield protecting his comrades. A bodyguard must be willing to make the ultimate sacrifice. It is an idea which has been adopted in terrorism by suicide-bombers who believe their gesture is for the greater good, much as there were Kamikaze pilots in World War II.

- **Symbols.** The archetypal shapes of heart, circle, cross/crucifix etc almost require no comment since we know these shapes. Some have even become emojis! We might all send a heart to a friend – no words are required as the image portrays the message and the feeling associated with it. Think of Valentine's Day. These images could all be amplified with cultural and historical data going back to the beginnings of life. Prehistoric cave paintings from ancient civilisations contain the same shapes/images as we draw nowadays. A recent example that has been discovered in a cave in Spain is of the 40,000-year-old outline of a hand. Hasn't every child drawn round their hand?

More broadly, 'symbolic' is the word used to denote a metaphorical image. The symbol exemplifies what is being expressed: "The moon is symbolic of all things feminine", or "the cat symbolically represents my feline nature".

People create their own mythologies, which nowadays can take the form of tattoos so that people are almost literally nailing their colours to the mast by covering their bodies in symbols which have both archetypal and/or personal significance.

The Archive for Research in Archetypal Symbolism is a wonderful resource to explore symbolic imagery. They have amassed a treasure trove of imagery going back to the beginning of time accompanied by scholarly narratives amplifying the meaning of each and cross-referencing to other images (ARAS 2010 and http://aras.org/).

ARCHETYPAL EVENTS

Predominantly we have been looking at archetypes as they manifest in the psychology of individuals. Archetypal events are often collective events too such as war, pillaging/rape, starvation, terrorism. Their form changes over time, but essentially these events are ubiquitous and have occurred since time immemorial. They have a numinous power which is why they have such a grip over us when we encounter them. You can often remember precisely where you were at such moments. We all remember the sight of the Twin Towers collapsing in New York on 11th September 2001. Perhaps even recall the visceral feeling of horror that accompanied the sight. Soldiers create lifetime bonds with their peers by fighting side by side and opening themselves to the possibility of losing their lives in combat. Soldiers are sometimes haunted by the damage wrought upon them by the act of killing. Again, film is a useful analogy. The canon is full of films about war of every type. We are gripped by these archetypal images.

The death of a monarch or person of great acclaim can create monumental turmoil in a populace as a whole. The death of Princess Diana is a case in point. The sudden nature of her death took the world by storm and affected most Britons, whether monarchists or not. The shock was palpable and sent ripples out widely. She embodied the archetype of the princess and her ability to move was thus greater than it would have been had she been a private individual. People who met her spoke about memories of encountering her as if she was a living saint whose touch could heal. See Haynes and Shearer (Eds) (1998) for a selection of papers by Jungian analysts on the aftermath of this event.

IDENTIFYING WITH ARCHETYPES

Although we need to own the unconscious aspects contained within some of the archetypes mentioned above, it is dangerous to actually identify with the archetypes as their powerful nature can lead to inflation. If you identify as being a 'Hero', you could get yourself into dangerous situations – think of Indiana Jones in *Raiders of the Lost Ark* (Dir: Steven Spielberg 1981). While many of us have heroic character traits, it is too much to see oneself as a Hero. Life would be too one-sided and have no scope for the more vulnerable qualities which keep us safe and in check. There is a danger of *la folie de grandeur* in being over-identified with the image or becoming prey to it. It creates ego mania and is associated with narcissism. Examples would be actors who fall prey to addictions when it becomes impossible to live up to the stardom with which they identify and indeed which is put on them when they are idealised by fans. It is too much to live up to. Or mothers who cannot let go of their children as they become adults because, without being needed as the nurturing mother any longer, they experience a loss of identity. Or pop singers who live the rock and roll lifestyle and cannot switch off and live a more ordinary life. It is difficult to let go of these identities even when they cause us harm.

MEANING

As mentioned above, 'meaning' as an idea is conceived of as an archetype. Perhaps meaning is something that is usually in the background and which in itself is not thought about. The act of acquiring meaning is a fundamental requirement in getting through life and making sense of what we experience. Without being able to make meaning, we would be ill; utterly disorientated. Samuels *et al* emphasise the centrality of meaning: "Meaning was fundamental to Jung's concept of the aetiology of neurosis since the *recognition of meaning appears to have a curative power*" (1986 p.92; my emphasis). This is a profoundly meaningful assertion. Meaning is central in Jung's thinking and philosophical standpoint: "A psychoneurosis must be understood, ultimately, as the suffering of a soul which has not discovered its meaning" (Jung 1932 par. 497).

Dale Mathers (Jungian analyst in the UK) states:

> [w]e are... meaning-making mammals, living in a complex eco-system of social networks. The functions of Self (agency, coherence, continuity and affective relating) depend on being continually able to retune meaning-making to link with new meaning-patterns in these ever-changing relational networks.
>
> (2001 p.117)

Mathers goes on:

> Our capacity to form and use myth lets us make symbols out of anything that comes along. This speaks of a deep, inborn need to give meaning in our lives. We are meaning-making animals. We

have to develop meaning, because survival of infancy and successful
socialisation depend on it. Meaning is an archetypal experience,
we can't help making it: in paranoid states we may wish we could,
in depressive states we *know* we can't. In either position, meaning
collapses.

(ibid. p.177)

Imagine for a moment a world without meaning.
What a nightmare that would be.

SUMMARY

We have looked at various archetypal images such as: Anima/us,
Mother/Father/Child, Shadow (including the Witch), Hero, Trickster,
Laughter, Number, Slavery, Love (in its many guises) and archetypal
events. We then looked at the archetype of meaning.

COMPLEXES

The unconscious is filled with complexes, at the heart of which
there is an archetypal core. Jungians speak of a mother complex or a
father complex, by which is meant that the presenting problem has
the archetype of the mother/father at its centre and issues might
manifest in a variety of ways which all radiate out from the archetypal core. Jung developed his theory of complexes in his work at
the Burghölzli Clinic in Switzerland, where he was developing his
Word Association Test from as early as 1902. He would read out a
list of words and the patient's response, associations and response
time were noted by an assistant. The results of these tests were
analysed and it was possible to discern emotional affect associated
with particular words and by the brevity or pause in the response
time. Jung then found that clusters of words which produced affect
would constellate around particular topics, which he came to think
of as feeling-toned complexes that then became abbreviated to
'complexes'.

   An example of working with a complex from clinical practice
would be the following which relates to a complex of loss and
abandonment:

Simon was a 40-year-old man who presented in therapy having recently broken up from his partner of seven years. He was filled with grief, which was causing him concern at work as his emotions were brimming over and affecting his ability to function. It emerged that Simon had lost his mother at an early age and the break-up was triggering grief from the original loss which he had never dealt with at depth. As he explored these issues we pieced together that his mother had died when Simon was seven and it seemed impossible for him to remain in a relationship for more than seven years when, on a deeply unconscious level, he anticipated the abandonment he had suffered as a child and unconsciously 'created' the ending which seemed ineluctable, or unavoidable. Identifying this pattern broke the impasse and enabled Simon to persevere beyond the stuckness that arose when he got to seven years in a relationship and when he came to a point beyond which he was in unknown territory emotionally and psychologically.

Another example:

Celia was a middle-aged woman who had been in therapy for many years before she began to notice that she and all her friends had similar life experiences to a most peculiar degree. She was aware that her friend Shoshi had been ousted from her own family many years ago after a youthful rebellion. She discovered Liza had experienced a similar distancing when she married a man of whom her family did not approve. Then she learnt that Clara had been cut out of her parents' Wills because they believed sons should inherit the family wealth. It was not until she learnt that her friend Georgio was in a similar state of disconnection from his family (having come out as gay) that she noticed they all had stories which were so similar at their core. This increased the depth of relationships within the friendship circle so that these painful circumstances created something positive. However, Celia was dealing with a complex resulting from repeated abandonment and that very trauma was discernable in so many areas of her life meaning it was virtually impossible to ignore this issue.

POST-JUNGIAN THINKING

The theory of the archetypes has been considerably revised since Jung's day. Post-Jungians have developed quite varied conceptions of the term 'archetype', ranging from the biological or instinctive pole (Knox 2003) to the imaginal or spiritual pole (Hillman 1989). Jean Knox (Jungian analyst in the UK) has revised archetypal theory to accommodate attachment theory (2003) whereas James Hillman (1926–2011) is the founding father of Archetypal Psychology, which is a development or offshoot of Analytical Psychology which sees archetypes as 'gods' in a metaphorical sense. Hillman was a charismatic speaker and poetic writer who became the director of studies at the C. G. Jung Institute in Zurich in 1959 before returning to the United States where he became Graduate Dean at the University of Dallas. He was a prolific writer and original thinker.

For Andrew Samuels (Professor of Analytical Psychology at the University of Essex who invented the term 'post-Jungians' [1985]), "archetypal theory provides a crucial link in the dialogues between nature and nurture, inner and outer, scientific and metaphorical, personal and collective or societal" (1985 p.23).

For Stevens and Price, archetypes are "conceived as neuropsychic units which evolved through natural selection and which are responsible for determining the behavioural characteristics as well as the affective and cognitive experiences typical of human beings" (1996, p.6).

For Michael Vannoy Adams in the US:

> the psyche is mythopoetic. It is intrinsically myth-making. It spontaneously and autonomously generates myths – or mythic images. It does so in modern times just as it did in ancient times. Only now we know that the "labyrinth" is the unconscious (see the cover of my book The Mythological Unconscious, which is a reproduction of Andre Masson's surrealist drawing "Minotaur and Labyrinth," which situates the labyrinth inside the minotaur – that's "interiority.")
>
> (Letter from Michael Vannoy Adam to International Association for Jungian Studies online discussion list, 29 April 2007)

Joe Cambray talks about the potential of an archetype emerging rather than being pre-existing. He discusses Wolfgang Pauli (1900–58), Nobel Laureate physicist and pioneer of quantum physics who worked with Jung on the theory of synchroncity:

Pauli was also helping to stress the shift in conception of the archetype away from being inborn or being an ideal form to something active, constellating rather than causing events... Thus the concept is moving toward an emergentist view.

(2009 p.29)

George Hogenson too has written about the archetype in the light of emergence theory. He states:

[E]mergence is based on the notion that within certain kinds of system, phenomena can come into being without any precursor state predicting the appearance of those phenomena.

(2004 p.45)

Archetypes do not 'exist' somewhere in the psyche in a pre-existing state. They are not objects in a concrete sense, but arise or emerge as needed.

SUMMARY

We have looked at a range of post-Jungian thinkers and how they each conceive of the archetypes. These include: Knox, Hillman, Samuels, Stevens & Price, Vannoy Adams, Cambray and Hogenson.

ARCHETYPAL ASTROLOGY

As early as 1911 Jung was exploring astrology as he intuited that it held the key to psychological truths and, while he even used it in a clinical context, I think it is fair to say that he was reluctant to emphasise his interest in astrology as he was keen to present himself as an empirical scientist. Astrology has never had very good press and is easily ridiculed. This is despite the fact that some of the greatest figures in Western thought had an interest in it: Plato, Aristotle, Ptolemy, Plotinus, Albertus Magnus, Thomas Aquinas, Dante, Ficino, Kepler, Goethe and Yeats (Tarnas 2006 p.63).

Richard Tarnas (Harvard-trained philosopher) and Stanislav Grof (founder of transpersonal psychology), in their 30-year collaboration, have together formulated a system they call archetypal astrology, which explores the connection between planetary patterns in the solar system and archetypal patterns in human experience. This is well worth exploring as their findings are profound and interesting.

Liz Greene is the queen of the psychological approach to astrology. She founded the Centre for Psychological Astrology in 1983 and continues as its director. She is a Jungian analyst and therefore brings her deep experience of analytical psychology to the practice of astrology. She has published widely and most recently has made a masterful study of the deep connections to astrology within Jung's *The Red Book* (2009) and in turn his influence on the practice of astrology itself (Greene 2018a and 2018b).

SUMMARY

The theory of archetypes has been discussed by reference to its definition and structure, followed by post-Jungian thinking, including how the theory of emergence has been introduced to explain their existence. We have looked at the archetype of meaning before exploring a range of archetypes and archetypal events. Their central place in the theory of complexes has been introduced.

Archetypes are instinct, innate, irrepresentable, bipolar and metaphorical. We then touched on the relatively new field of archetypal astrology.

REFERENCES

ARAS (2010) *The Book of Symbols: Reflections on Archetypal Images*. Köln: Taschen.
Austen, J. (1996 [1813]) *Pride & Prejudice*. London & New York: Penguin Classics.
Barrie, J.M. (1980 [1911]) *Peter Pan*. New York: Atheneum Books.
Brewster, F. (2017) *African Americans and Jungian Psychology: Leaving the Shadows*. London & New York: Routledge.
Bronte, E. (1995 [1847]) *Wuthering Heights*. London & New York: Penguin Books.
Buck, C. & Lee, J. (2013) *Frozen*. Walt Disney Animation Studios.
Cambray, J. (2009) *Synchronicity: Nature and Psyche in an Interconnected Universe*. College Station, TX: Texas A&M University Press.
Christian Anderson, H. (2015 [1844]) *The Snow Queen*. London: Hutchinson.
Curtiz, M. (Dir) (1942) *Casablanca*. Warner Bros.
Dahl, J. et al (Dir) (2006–13) *Dexter* (Series 1–8). Showtime Networks.
Fielding, H. (1996) *Bridget Jone's Diary*. London: Picador.

von Franz, M-L. (1974) *Number and Time*. London: Rider & Company.

von Franz, M-L. (1995) *Shadow and Evil in Fairy Tales*. Boston, MA: Shambhala.

Greene, L. (2018a) *The Astrological World of Jung's Liber Novus: Daimons, Gods and the Planetary Journey*. London & New York: Routledge.

Greene, L. (2018b) *Jung's Studies in Astrology: Prophecy, Magic, and the Qualities of Time*. London & New York: Routledge.

Haynes, J. & Shearer, A. (1998) *When a Princess Dies: Reflections from Jungian Analysts*. London: Harvest Books.

Heckerling, A. (Dir.) (1995) *Clueless*. Paramount Pictures.

Hillman, J. (1989) *A Blue Fire*. New York: Harper Perennial.

Hogenson, G. (2004) "Archetypes: Emergence and the psyche's deep structure" in *Analytical Psychology: Contemporary Perspectives in Jungian Analysis*. (Ed. J. Cambray & L. Carter). Hove & New York: Brunner-Routledge, pp.32–55.

Homer (1946) *The Odyssey*. Harmondsworth: Penguin Classics.

Jung, C.G. (1902) "On the Psychology and Pathology of So-called Occult Phenomena" in *CW1*.

Jung, C.G. (1931) "Marriage as a Psychological Relationship" in CW17.

Jung, C.G. (1932) "Psychotherapists or the Clergy" in CW11.

Jung, C.G. (1944) *Psychology and Alchemy in* CW12.

Jung, C.G. (1946) "Psychology of the Transference" in CW16.

Jung, C.G. (1948) "A Psychological Approach to the Dogma of the Trinity" in CW11.

Jung, C.G. (1949a) "Foreward to Harding: '*Woman's Mysteries*'" in CW18.

Jung, C.G. (1949b) "Foreword to Neumann: 'Depth Psychology and a New Ethic'" in CW18.

Jung, C.G. (1951) *Aion*, CW9ii.

Jung, C.G. (1954a) "Psychological Aspects of the Mother Archetype" in CW9i.

Jung, C.G. (1954b) "On the Nature of the Psyche" in CW8.

Jung, C.G. (1954c) "Concerning the Archetypes, with Special Reference to the Anima Concept" in CW9i.

Jung, C.G. (1956) "Recent Thoughts on Schizophrenia" in CW3.

Jung, C.G. (1973) *C.G. Jung Letters. Vol. 1: 1906–1950*. (Ed. G. Adler & E. Jaffé; Trans. R.F.C. Hull). London: Routledge & Kegan Paul.

Knowles, B. (2008) "If I Were a Boy" from *I Am… Sasha Fierce* (album). RCA Records.

Knox, J. (2003) *Archetype, Attachment, Analysis: Jungian Psychology and the Emergent Mind*. Hove: Brunner-Routledge.

MacLaren, M. *et al* (Dir: M. MacLaren *et al* 2008–13) *Breaking Bad* (Seasons 1–5). Sony Pictures.

Mathers, D. (2001) *An Introduction to Meaning and Purpose in Analytical Psychology*. Hove & Philadelphia, PA: Brunner-Routledge.

Neumann, E. (1955) *The Great Mother: An Analysis of the Archetype.* London: Routledge & Kegan Paul.

Potter, S. (Dir) (1993) *Orlando.* Adventure Pictures et al.

Rowling, J.K. (2014) *Harry Potter and the Philosopher's Stone* (1 of 7 [Harry Potter 1]). London: Bloomsbury Publishing.

Samuels, A. (1985) *Jung and the Post-Jungians.* London & New York: Routledge, 1997.

Samuels, A. (1998) "Her Body Politic" in *When a Princess Dies: Reflections from Jungian Analysts.* (Ed. J. Haynes & A. Shearer). London: Harvest Books, pp. 37–45.

Samuels, A. *et al* (1986) *A Critical Dictionary of Jungian Analysis.* London & New York: Routledge, 1997.

Shamdasani, S. (Ed.) (2009) *The Red Book: Liber Novus. C. G. Jung.* London: W.W. Norton & Company.

Spielberg, S. (Dir.) (1981) "Raiders of the Lost Ark". Paramount Films.

Stein, M. & Shalit, E. (Eds.) (2016) *Turbulent Times, Creative Minds: Erich Neumann and C.G. Jung in Relationship (1933–1960).* Asheville, NC: Chiron Publications.

Stevens, A. (2006) "The Archetypes" in R. K. Papadopoulos (Ed.) *The Handbook of Jungian Psychology – Theory, Practice and Applications.* London & New York Routledge. pp. 74–93.

Stevens, A. & Price, J. (1996) *Evolutionary Psychiatry: A New Beginning.* London: Routledge.

Tarnas, R. (2006) *Cosmos and Psyche: Intimations of a New World View.* London: Penguin Viking.

Wilhelm, R. (Trans.) (1942) *The Secret of the Golden Flower: A Chinese Book of Life.* London: Kegan Paul, Trench, Trubner & Co Ltd.

Wilhelm, R. (Trans.) (1951) *I Ching (or Book of Changes).* London, Melbourne & Henley: Routledge & Kegan Paul.

Williams, R. (2017) *Festschrift of The Association of Jungian Analysts. 40th Anniversary.* London: AJA.

Woolf, V. (2016 [1928]) *Orlando.* London: Vintage Classics Woolf Series.

RESOURCES

Archive for Research in Archetypal Symbolism: http://aras.org/

4

INDIVIDUATION

OUTLINE

Individuation is the term Jung adopted to describe the lifelong process of becoming oneself. This might sound rather odd at first sight
in that who else can we be? Other depth psychologists agree we
have defensive behaviours to cope with which obscure our nature
and inhibit fuller expression of our authentic selves. This may cause
us to develop what Winnicott termed a false self, whereby we create
a form of persona as an adaptation to present to the world; to hide
behind. (Donald Winnicott was an influential English paediatrician and psychoanalyst). What Jung uniquely articulates is that we
have a purposive function in life and can consciously work towards
becoming more 'ourselves'. Living consciously is our form of
individuation:

> A plant that is meant to produce a flower is not individuated if it
> does not produce a flower... and the man who does not develop
> consciousness is not individuated, because consciousness is his
> flower – it is his life.

> (Jung 1998 p.759)

Individuation is a process of transformation involving both conscious intent to change and develop as well as unconscious drives (see Chapter 1) differentiating what does and does not fit into our overall totality as a person. What is 'mine' or 'me' are questions we ask ourselves. Individuation is the process by which we become a separate psychological individual, distinct from all others. A spiritual dimension of this would be finding not only who we are as individuals, but finding a sense of purpose in life and fulfilling our potential. I have avoided using words such as fate and destiny here as they seem too monolithic but in a modest sense they could indeed be applied.

Man may have been born equal, but we are not the same and we do not all have the same destinies. Marie-Louise von Franz (a close colleague and collaborator of Jung) expresses it like this:

It is... useless to cast furtive glances at the way someone else is developing, because each of us has a unique task of self-realization. Although many human problems are similar, they are never identical. All pine trees are very much alike (otherwise we should not recognise them as pines), yet none is exactly the same as another. Because of these factors of sameness and difference, it is difficult to summarize the infinite variations of the process of individuation. The fact is that each person has to do something different, something that is uniquely his own.

(Marie-Louise von Franz quoted in Jung 1964 p.167)

Buddhists might view this process as a result of Karma (whereby we are reincarnated in different forms, which – although not a linear progress – implies a sense of transformation through different states until we achieve wholeness).

It does seem that we each have different tasks in life. The circumstances into which we are born dictate many factors in terms of what may be achieved, without touching on the nature/nurture debate or arguing about the relative effects of what we are intrinsically born with, and the environmental factors which influence our development and expectations. The nature-versus-nurture debate is important when it comes to thinking about how we develop. That conversation is now facilitated by the findings of the human genome project, which should in time provide greater evidence for understanding the proportional roles of environment versus biological heredity. (The Human Genome Project is an international scientific research project exploring the sequence of chemical base pairs which make up human DNA. They are identifying and mapping all of the genes of the human genome.) To date this project has focused on the concerns of physical health. We are yet to discover what it tells us about psychological health. Where do personality, emotional disposition or mental health issues originate?

Political factors can determine and influence the course of our lives, although these need not necessarily be the final word and may generate the energy to break through the 'glass ceiling' or limitations which seem to obstruct our progression at times. Many feel spiritually that we each have hoops to go through which, as time goes by, can seem as if they have a pattern. This is how we learn and grow.

Family dynamics certainly play an important role. Birth order, being the favourite child, your gender all influence your place in a family. If there is trauma in a family such as having survived a war or becoming a refugee, these dynamics can and do effect generations of survivors in deep ways, which may initially look like personal troubles. These are the ways in which we are warped – or shaped – by life events. Donald Kalsched in the US published his seminal *The Inner World of Trauma: Archetypal Defences of the Personal Spirit* in 1996, which explores the interior life of people who have suffered unbearable trauma and outlines what he sees as a self-care system which may be adopted to counter such experiences. These are again ways in which we adapt to the environment (both inner and outer) and form our character and personality.

A succinct summary from *A Critical Dictionary of Jungian Analysis*:

> [Individuation] is the key concept of Jung's contribution to the theories of personality development. As such, it is inextricably interwoven with others, particularly Self, Ego and Archetype as well as with the synthesis of consciousness and unconscious elements. A simplified way of expressing the relationship of the most important concepts involved would be: ego is to integration (socially seen as adaptation) what the self is for individuation (self-experience and –realisation). While consciousness is increased by the analysis of defences (eg projection of

the Shadow), the process of individuation is a circumambulation of the self as the centre of the personality which thereby becomes unified....
[T]he person becomes conscious in what respects he or she is both a unique human being and, at the same time, no more than a common man or woman.

(Samuels *et al* 1986 p.76)

Jung uses the term individuation: "to denote the process by which a person becomes a psychological 'in-dividual', that is, a separate, indivisible unity or 'whole'" (1939 para. 490). This is quite different from individualism, which is ego-led (as opposed to Self-led individuation). It is an attempt to mark oneself out as different, which may well be necessary at times. Acting from the 'Self' is regarded as an achievement as the path towards individuation involves an enhancement of the personality, which builds a greater sense of who we are as unique individuals.

Individuation is not a process to be forced or induced any more than you can rip a seedling out of the ground to hurry along its growth. Both have to unfold organically, some might say *Deo Condecente* (by the grace of God). Individuation points to the process, Jung tells us, whereby: "the acorn becomes an oak, the calf a cow, and the child an adult" (1952 par. 755). It is the unfolding of our destiny. By this I do not intend to imply that it is inevitable that we follow the path of our destiny. Many people never find their purpose in life. It involves arduous psychological work to find and incarnate the paths in life which we need to follow to fulfil our potential.

GATE DIAGRAM

Perhaps paradoxically Jung spoke about individuation as taking place in the relationship with others. He saw the process of analysis as dialectical, something going on between the two individuals, as opposed to being akin to an expert doctor telling his patient what the problem is, the more traditional medical model. Rather than being a hierarchical relationship, Jung regarded analysis – as do contemporary analysts – as a relationship of equals in which both contribute to the process and both gain. He created what is sometimes called his gate diagram to illustrate this process (1946 par. 422). Because he

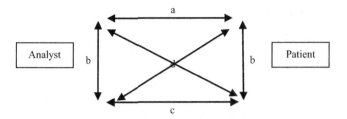

Figure 4.1   Gate diagram

uses arcane language to illustrate his meaning in the original, I have adapted the diagram using English in Figure 4.1.

Figure 4.1 indicates how, in Jung's view, the relationship exerts influence between the two individuals in every conceivable direction (even when you feel yourself to be quite powerless). The horizontal line 'a' refers to the conscious to conscious relationship of which we are overtly aware; horizontal line 'c' refers to the unconscious to unconscious relationship. The two vertical lines marked 'b' represent the analyst on one side and the patient on the other (although this applies to all relationships). The lines denote how in a relationship we are constantly relating to each other on all these different planes. The crossed lines marked 'd' point to how the unconscious of one person can relate to or communicate with the conscious of another. My conscious statement can hook into something in you quite unconsciously, and by the same token an unconscious communication can be picked up by the other party in a conscious way. Naturally, a conscious communication may be received in a conscious way. So far, so relatively straightforward, although it might be helpful to take some time to stay with this diagram and imagine how it could have played out in a situation you have been in. What might be a novel idea is the unconscious can just as well communicate with another party's unconscious. I anticipate you might say "how could you know?" The answer to this is that unconscious communications can rise up into awareness, and the work of analysis is to notice when this happens. We become more aware by interpreting unconscious communications such as parapraxes (more usually referred to as Freudian slips), 'aha' moments, or in dreams (see Chapter 5).

STAGES OF LIFE

Individuation will manifest differently at the various stages of life. Individuation is intended to connote more than a person's literal development in years. Jung wrote a seminal paper on "The Stages of Life" (1931 paras. 749–95) (which can also be found in *Modern Man in Search of a Soul*, regarded as a classic and is a good place to start reading Jung). He compares the stages to the sun:

> The one hundred and eighty degrees of the arc of life are divisible into four parts. The first quarter, lying to the east, is childhood, that state in which we are a problem for others but are not yet conscious of any problems of our own. Conscious problems fill out the second and third quarters; while in the last, in extreme old age, we descend again into that condition where, regardless of our state of consciousness, we once more become something of a problem for others.
>
> (ibid. par. 795)

He broke down the stages of life we all go through in the following way:

- **Infancy and childhood** is a time of tremendous growth not only physically, but in developing an ego. That is, a sense of 'I' evolves. Ego has to do with reality-testing, orienting ourselves as to where we fit into the world. This is a period for remaining dependent upon parents or caregivers and building up emotional resilience, which will facilitate dealing with future challenges.
- **Adolescence and early adulthood** involves the process of psychological separation from the mother. There are tasks to be achieved. During this phase people think about finding a partner, having children and creating one's own family and home, how to earn a living. Psychic birth and differentiation from the parents tends to occur around puberty.
- **Adulthood and midlife.** Gaining an adult identity is profoundly important in being able to function fully during this phase of life. This will usually involve attaining a social position, a friendship group, possibly a career. The emphasis in life is here often shifting from an external focus (in terms of acquisition of material status and family and so forth), to a more reflective one in terms of relationship to the Self, searching for meaning in life and recognising

what is important to a person, often bringing spiritual seeking to the fore.

- **Maturity and wisdom.** Jung likens this phase to the setting sun. Thoughts inevitably turn towards death as the end of life appears on the horizon.

These categories seem quite unremarkable or obvious, but in fact Jung was preeminent in formulating a theory which drew attention to the differing needs and tasks of each stage of life: "we cannot live the afternoon of life according to the programme of life's morning: for what was great in the morning will be little at evening, and what in the morning was true will at evening have become a lie" (ibid. par. 784).

SUMMARY

The key stages of life are divided into:

- Childhood
- Adolescence and early adulthood
- Adulthood and midlife
- Maturity and wisdom

DEVELOPMENTAL MODEL

Developmental psychology is concerned with how and why human beings develop over the course of their life. Originally the prime focus was on infants and children, but the field has expanded to include adolescence and adult development. This is where the question of nature/nurture enters the field: what is innate and what is acquired by environmental influence from other familial or external factors? It asks whether we are genetically bound to develop in particular ways, or whether there is some choice involved: destiny or fate?

Major figures whose ideas have been incorporated into a Developmental approach in Jungian analysis and who merit attention are as follows:

MICHAEL FORDHAM (1905–95)

Michael Fordham in London pioneered the evolution of the Developmental model and was the leading force in creating what has come to be known as the Developmental School (see Samuels 1985 Chapter 1 pp.1–22), sometimes referred to as the London School (although actually the Jungian analysts in London encompass various approaches of which this is but one). Fordham co-edited the Collected Works of C.G. Jung with Gerhard Adler and Sir Herbert Read, and was a leader in setting up the Society of Analytical Psychology (the first London Jungian society) to train clinicians interested in Jung's ideas. He made significant contributions to analytic theory and practice, extending its scope to include the Jungian analysis of children.

The Developmental School integrates Jungian ideas to include those extended and expanded by later generations of analysts following Jung known as post-Jungians, with those of psychoanalysis and other practitioners and theorists in analysis and psychotherapy more broadly such as attachment theory and the recent advances in neuroscience as they relate to the field. Fordham's ideas deconstruct the journey the child and baby undergo in the process of developing into full beings. His most radical departure from Jung was to describe the actions of the self in infancy and childhood such that the infant, far from being uncentred at birth, as Jung originally thought, is a person with an individual identity even in utero. (See www.thesap.org.uk/resources/articles-on-jungian-psychology-2/michael-fordham/ [accessed 30 May 2016] and *Michael Fordham: Innovations in Analytical Psychology*, by James Astor, 1995.)

MELANIE KLEIN (1882–1960)

Melanie Klein, born in Vienna, is one of the towering figures in contemporary psychoanalysis. Building on the theories of Sigmund Freud, she recognised the centrality of the infant's early relationships with his or her primary caregivers and elucidated – or descriptively imagined – the early mental processes that build up a person's internal world. She took infancy seriously. A pioneering child analyst, she was a controversial and powerful member of the British Psychoanalytical Society for 30 years. To this day there are a whole group of psychoanalysts who follow her.

Klein's observation of children's play led her to explore their preoccupation with what went on both internally and how they experienced others as they interact with the outside world. 'Internal object' is the term used in Kleinian theory to refer to an inner mental and emotional image of an external figure, together with the experience of that figure. The inner world is conceptualised as being populated by internal objects; the external world contains external objects. Her approach has thus come to be known as Object Relations. (See www.melanie-klein-trust.org.uk/home [accessed 30 May 2016]). Klein's language can seem somewhat negative but in fact her ideas are highly original and of great value clinically.

Klein places great importance on Freud's concept of transference – the conscious and unconscious expression of past and present experiences, relationships, thoughts, phantasies and feelings, both positive and negative, in relation to the analyst. (Note that Klein deliberately refers to 'phantasy' to denote an internal *imago* to differentiate it from the more usual 'fantasy', which refers to daydream images and imagination.) Klein's followers have developed her techniques further by placing greater emphasis on the analyst–patient relationship and in the use of countertransference, the corresponding, reciprocal experience of the analyst which provides a rich seam of information with which to understand the patient (c.f. Jung's gate diagram (adapted) in Figure 4.1, p.65).

DONALD WINNICOTT (1896–1971)

Donald Winnicott was a London-based paediatrician who studied psychoanalysis with Melanie Klein. He said we cannot think about the development of any child in isolation from the external environment, in particular the relationship with parental figures. His writing is very accessible to read. Key ideas are:

- The Transitional Object: Such as the teddy bear or soggy blanket which babies invest with tremendous meaning/importance, the attachment to which Winnicott saw as serving a vital function for children in creating a sense of security.
- The good-enough mother: The good-enough mother is someone who makes mistakes and can be seen as fallible, but who is also able to repair mistakes and demonstrate they are not the end of

the world. This is seen as providing a vital 'holding' environment in which the child learns how to cope with his or her own frailties and mistakes.

- True self, false self: c/f Jung's persona (see Chapter 2). The Winnicottian false self develops in response to failures of empathy in the parent or the infant's environment such as misattunement, abandonment or lack of love. It is a defence mechanism used to cope with these deficiencies.
- Development stages: Winnicott broke down the stages of development into unity, transition, independence.
- Play: Winnicott invented a technique he called the Squiggle game, which he used when working with children. He would make a 'squiggle', a twisted or wiggly line spontaneously drawn on a piece of paper. The child would then add elements to the drawing, and the analyst and child would comment on its meaning. The analyst then transforms the child's drawing, and the analyst and child further comment on the drawing. This interview diagnostic is based on the idea of testing a therapeutic response. Winnicott saw play as deeply transformative.

(See http://changingminds.org/disciplines/psychoanalysis/theorists/winnicott.htm, accessed 30 May 2016).

JOHN BOWLBY (1907–90)

Attachment theory was developed by John Bowlby, a psychiatrist and psychoanalyst best known for his work on the effects of separating infants and young children from their mothers. He collaborated with James Robertson in the production of a film, *A Two-Year Old Goes to the Hospital* (1952), which graphically illustrated the distressing effects of separation. His major works were a trilogy on *Attachment* (1969), *Separation* (1973) and *Loss* (1980).

The dominant themes in his approach are rejection of classical (ie Freudian) drive theory, emphasis on the importance of environmental factors – particularly relationships, the crucial place of mourning, and the link between attachment, security and exploration. Attachment theory is a response to the need to develop new approaches to the relationship between the emotional world of the

psyche and the relational milieu. (See http://thebowlbycentre.org.
uk/, accessed 30 May 2016.)

Training as an analyst or psychotherapist in a Developmental model
often includes an infant observation lasting a year or more. A mother
with a newborn is visited in their home for weekly observations
to witness at close hand the intricate shifts which take place in the
development of the baby and the relationship they are building with
their caregivers and siblings. Most trainees find this a moving experience and privilege.

Of these theoreticians, only Fordham is a Jungian. Klein, Winnicott
and Bowlby's ideas were drawn together in this nexus forming the
Developmental model in an attempt to bridge the differences with
Freudian psychoanalysis. Although this model is predominantly
associated with London, it has wider prominence worldwide.

SUMMARY

We have reviewed the Developmental approach with particular
attention on the following who have made significant contributions
to this field:

Michael Fordham
Melanie Klein
Donald Winnicott
John Bowlby

CLASSICAL AND ARCHETYPAL APPROACHES

In Samuels' seminal *Jung and the Post-Jungians* (1985) he postulates a
tripartite division in the different approaches to Jungian schools of
thinking, which he describes as follows:

- Developmental
- Classical
- Archetypal

There are cross-overs between these strands so that people may
well be influenced or see themselves as falling within more than
one of these categories. The Archetypal School never really caught

on as a clinical model although the ideas are applied in arenas such as Jungian film studies. The Archetypal School expanded its base in Jungian psychology to incorporate such influences as French philosopher Henry Corbin (1903–78), Italian Enlightenment philosopher Giambattista Vico (1668–1744) and the Greek-speaking philosopher from the ancient world, born in Egypt in AD 204, Plotinus, among others. Preeminent among writers in the Archetypal School is James Hillman (1926–2011), who wrote prolifically on a wide range of topics. His writing is very easy to access and many of his books read like poetry. Others of note within this School are Roberto Gambini in Brazil, Rafael López-Pedraza (1920–11) (originally from Cuba), Hayao Kawai (1928–2007) (who introduced Jungian psychology to Japan), and Patricia Berry (one of the founders of the Archetypal School with James Hillman) who is on the faculty of the Pacifica Graduate Institute in California.

The Classical School is the approach taught in Zurich in particular (Jung's birthplace and home), where there is a lively international centre of Jungian Studies and training. As in Jung's own days, people travel to Zurich from all over the world to study his ideas. The approach of the Classical School is centred on working predominantly with dreams, myth and fairy tales (see Chapter 5 'Psychological types' for an example of this thinking). There is a rich interchange of ideas between practitioners of myths and stories from every culture in the world, which may be applied either clinically or in looking at psychosocial or cultural issues. Many images may be studied in depth at ARAS (The Archive for Research in Archetypal Symbolism; https://aras.org/), a fantastic resource which has been collecting and cataloguing images for 80 years. They archive photographic images, which are placed alongside scholarly commentary to include a description of the image with a cultural history that serves to place it in its unique historical and geographical setting. Often it also includes an archetypal commentary that analyses its modern psychological and symbolic meaning. Important writers to mention in relation to the Classical School are Verena Kast (1943–), Marie-Louise von Franz (1915–98), and Edward Edinger 1922–98), all of whom are widely published and well worth searching out. Also of note is Marion Woodman (1928–2018), who has published many bestsellers which are very readable. This is a small selection of the vast array of publications available and I mean no disrespect to any of the writers not mentioned.

If you think myth is dry and dusty and something you would not relate to personally, I would recommend the multi-award-winning rap poet Kate Tempest who has single-handedly created a genre where she has brought myth into the 21st century. Her *Brand New Ancients* (2013) (both poetry book and album), for which she won the prestigious Ted Hughes Prize for innovation in poetry, is a *tour de force* filled with wit and emotion. For the cover she has used an image which at first glance looks like an ancient Greek vase. On closer inspection, the figures walking across the image are carrying a Tesco carrier bag, a briefcase, a can of beer, and the woman holds an iPod linked to earphones. (It is well worth watching her perform the poem either online or live on stage if you can.)

I should emphasise that I have highlighted areas where Jungian psychology may be studied as clinical praxis. Jung is also taught in universities in the UK, US, Italy, Brazil, China and Taiwan and elsewhere, and in English-language universities in 'applied' contexts (such as religious studies, comparative literature, interdisciplinary studies etc).

SUMMARY

We have discussed the Archetypal and Classical Schools, looking at their formation, influences and key writers.

ACTIVE IMAGINATION AND *THE RED BOOK*

One of the methods Jung developed for working on the individuation process he came to call Active Imagination; the Classical School would also incorporate this method. This was something which spontaneously sprung from his personal, inner struggles during a period beginning around 1913–18. Jung was highly creative and an accomplished artist. He found ways to process issues from playing with stones which he built into elaborate structures, carving stone sculptures and painting. This period from around 1913 has been described by Jung's detractors as a psychotic breakdown (see Sedgwick 2008). I would suggest it was a sustained period of working matters through during which he went into unknown territory emotionally and psychically, which took him to the edge of a breakdown. However, throughout this period he continued his medical practice and had an active family life with a wife and children, and clearly functioned in a coherent fashion. Jung regarded this period as supremely important. He wrote:

> The years... when I pursued the inner images, were the most important time of my life. Everything else is to be derived from this. It began at that time, and the later details hardly matter anymore. My entire life consisted in elaborating what had burst forth from the unconscious and flooded me like an enigmatic stream and threatened to break me. That was the stuff and material for more than only one life. Everything later was merely the outer classification, the scientific elaboration, and the integration into life. But the numinous beginning, which contained everything, was then.
>
> (1957 from the protocols of Aniela Jaffé's interviews with Jung for *Memories, Dreams, Reflections*, Library of Congress, Washington DC. [original in German]; Shamdasani (Ed.) 2009)

Jung has written about the dreams – perhaps visions – he had during this time, which were published alongside a number of his paintings in 2009 in *The Red Book*. *The Red Book* does not form part of Jung's *Collected Works* where his theoretical writings are to be found (see *Jung The Collected Works: The Basics* by Lu and Yeoman [Routledge, forthcoming]). *The Red Book* is written in a highly experimental way using fantasies and a myth which he created in *The Red Book* as a metaphor to explore the unconscious. It is not an easy read and would certainly not be a place to start with Jung's writings.

It is much easier to begin with Jung's memoir, *Memories, Dreams, Reflections*, which was published posthumously in 1963 and recorded and edited by his colleague Aniela Jaffé. In his memoir some of the stories and dreams from *The Red Book* can be found. There are guides to help the intrepid reader find their way around this difficult text such as *Reading The Red Book: An Interpretive Guide to C.G. Jung's Liber Novus* (Drob 2012). Although *The Red Book* has been compared to major classics in world literature, some are embarrassed by the deeply personal nature of the fantasies and think it should have remained a private journal. Jung opens himself up in *The Red Book* so personally to expose the unfettered unconscious contents of his mind and shows himself as a man willing to risk everything to explore the greatest depths in the service of us all. He gives us a model of how we can ourselves explore our psyche —which from a Jungian perspective is intended to encompass the soul — at depth. What a gift this is.

The Red Book not only forms the map to Jung's own journey of individuation, but shows how he developed the process of Active Imagination. He grapples with the big questions in life such as the nature of reason, love and evil. The myth which Jung created in *The Red Book* centres around a character he called Philemon. Philemon appeared to Jung in a dream in 1913. Jung painted the image as a way of trying to glean some understanding of what the dream meant. Philemon became an important figure in Jung's fantasies, representing superior insight, and functioned as a kind of psychopomp or spiritual guide to Jung.

The overall theme of the book is how Jung regains his soul and overcomes the contemporary malaise of spiritual alienation. This is ultimately achieved through enabling the rebirth of a new image of God in his soul and developing a new worldview with a psychological and theological cosmology. *Liber Novus* presents the prototype of his conception of the individuation process, the universal form of individual psychological development. *Liber Novus* itself can be understood on the one hand as depicting Jung's individuation process, and as his elaboration of a general psychological schema. At the beginning of the book, Jung re-finds his soul and then embarks on a sequence of fantasy adventures, which form a consecutive narrative. He realised until then that he had served the spirit of the time, characterised by use and value. In addition to this, there existed a spirit of the depths, which led to matters of the soul (Shamdasani 2009 p.207).

Jung laid out his method of Active Imagination — which he described as dreaming with eyes open — in his final work as follows:

> [You] choose a dream, or some other fantasy-image, and concentrate on it by simply catching hold of it and looking at it.... Usually it will alter, as the mere fact of contemplating it animates it.... A chain of fantasy

ideas develops and gradually takes on a dramatic character: the passive process becomes an action. At first it consists of projected figures, and these images are observed like scenes in the theatre.... You dream with open eyes... If the observer understands that his own drama is being performed on this inner stage, he cannot remain indifferent to the plot and its dénouement. He will notice, as the actors appear one by one and the plot thickens, that they all have some purposeful relationship to his conscious situation.

(1944 par. 706)

Anecdotally, this method is somewhat akin to that practised by the Surrealists in Paris such as Andre Bretton set out in his *Manifestoes of Surrealism* (1924). They set up clinics where they invited people to enter into a spontaneous process of creativity. There are also similarities to the practice of automatic writing somewhat earlier. Psychology professor Théodore Flournoy (1854–1920), who was an early influence on Jung, investigated claims made by 19th-century medium Hélène Smith (Catherine Müller) that she used automatic writing to convey messages from Mars in Martian language (Flournoy 1900).

ACTIVE IMAGINATION AND *THE RED BOOK*

Active Imagination is a method Jung devised by using creativity to explore dream/fantasy images.

The Red Book is where Jung developed a new worldview in the form of a psychological and theological cosmology, using Active Imagination.

MANDALAS

Jung first mentions mandalas in his *Commentary on The Secret of the Golden Flower* (1957 pars. 1–84). A number of the images in *The Red Book* are mandalas. Mandalas, a Sanskrit word, are an ancient pattern (either square or circular or a combination of the two usually containing a quarternity – or patterns in the multiple of four – in the form of a cross, a star, a square in an octagon) which Jung thought as symbols of the Self. He described them as ideograms (or symbols) representing unconscious contents (1950a par.622). They naturally arise as images without any conscious act of will. Indeed, Jung went on:

> [o]ne can paint very complicated pictures without having the least idea of their real meaning. While painting them, the picture seems to develop out of itself and often in opposition to one's conscious intentions.
>
> (ibid.)

Jung clearly thought mandalas were significant:

> When I began drawing the mandalas, however, I saw that everything, all the paths I had been following, all the steps I had taken, were leading back to a single point – namely, to the mid-point. It became increasingly plain to me that the mandala is the centre. It is the exponent of all paths. It is the path to the centre, to individuation.
>
> (Jaffé 1963 p.222)

Even highly complicated mandalas have symmetry so it is noticeable when something is out of balance. Take some time to study the mandala which appears as a frontpiece (that is Mandala 105 from *The Red Book*). Gather together your own ideas about what it might represent before reading the next paragraph where Jung gives an indication of what he intended it to represent:

> In the centre, the white light, shining in the firmament; in the first circle, protoplasmic life-seeds; in the second, rotating cosmic principles which contain the four primary colours; in the third and fourth, creative forces working inward and outward. At the cardinal points, the masculine and feminine souls, both again divided into light and dark.
>
> (1957 A6)

In Tibetan Buddhism mandalas are used as a focus of concentration to assist meditation. Tibetan monks create mandalas out of single grains of coloured sand. The site to be used is consecrated with chants and music. Then, over a number of days, the monks create the design. The monks then enact the impermanent nature of existence by sweeping up the coloured grains and washing them away in flowing water. You will find film clips of these ceremonies online which are worth watching. The monks can be watched over the number of days it took to first create and then destroy a mandala.

Jung kept quiet about his developing ideas regarding the significance of mandalas for 13 years while he researched and studied many texts to discover such symbols had been painted, carved in stone, built and even danced in all ages and the world over. They are archetypal (see Chapter 3). He also found in his clinical work that mandalas appear in dreams. Here is an example. When first publishing this material Jung used the device of attributing the dream to a patient, but we now know that in fact it was his own. He painted an image of this dream in *The Red Book*. In the dream he is:

> with three young travelling companions in Liverpool. It was night and raining. The air was full of smoke and soot. They climbed up from the harbour to the "upper city". It was terribly dark and disagreeable, and we could not understand how anyone could stick it here... one of my companions said that remarkably enough, a friend of his had settled here... [w]e reached a sort of public garden in the middle of the city. The park was square, and in the centre was a lake or large pool. A few street lamps lit up the pitch darkness, and I could see a little island in the pool. On it there was a single tree, a red-flowering magnolia, which miraculously stood in everlasting sunshine. I noticed that my companions had not seen this miracle, whereas I was beginning to understand why the man had settled there.
>
> (1950b par. 654)

Note that the four characters mentioned form a quarternity, which itself would be significant in terms of it being conceived of as a mandala. In discussing this dream Jung writes:

> I tried to paint this dream. But as so often happens, it came out rather different. The magnolia turned into a sort of rose made of ruby-coloured glass. It shone like a four-rayed star. The square represents the wall of the park and at the same time a street leading round the park in a square. From it there radiate eight main streets, and from each of these eight side-streets, which meet in a shining red central point rather like the Etoile in Paris. The acquaintance mentioned in the dream lived in a house at the corner of one of these stars.
>
> (ibid. par. 655)

He interprets: "The mandala thus combines the classic motifs of flower, star, circle, precinct (*temenos*), and plan of city divided into quarters with citadel. The whole thing seemed like a window opening on to eternity" (ibid.). The painting itself can be found both in volume 9i of Jung's Collected Works as Figure 6 and in *The Red Book* at p.159.

Mandalas are ancient archetypal patterns/paintings (usually square or round), which may also appear in dreams and which Jung came to regard as symbols of the Self.

ARTS THERAPIES

When Jung used art in his clinical work, he would track the changes – the individuation process – through the art and pick up the evolving nature of the images and colours used to ascertain his client's state of mind. Art therapy has evolved into a modern profession and art therapists are part of multi-disciplinary teams in hospitals alongside psychiatrists, psychologists and others. Much can be gleaned even from the materials a patient uses (for example, are images drawn in colour or black and white? Can they make full use of all the materials on offer or do they need to be abstemious? Are they drawn in tiny fragments which are hard to even see, or on a large scale?). Sometimes the patient will take the image home after a session; others prefer to leave the image in the care of the therapist so that it is available for future reference. I would suggest, when the artwork is left in the care of the therapist, there is also a symbolic wish at these times to be held in the therapist's mind/heart.

A clinical vignette from working with a patient might help elucidate how these approaches work in practice. An extended case study can be found in Schaverien (1995 Chapter 4), which has the rare advantage of having a dual text sharing insights from both the practitioner and the patient. The text is interspersed with the many drawings and paintings produced by the patient who had been hospitalised as a result of an eating disorder. He experienced the art therapy as a release. The images communicated to the therapist that there was a reticence to allow mess. The therapist inferred that "the yearning for neatness, order and detail is a form of control of passion" (ibid. p.62), which it can probably be imagined might have a significant link to an eating disorder where intake of food has to be controlled. This tiny snippet is only intended to give a taste of the method. I will leave the last word to the patient himself who Schaverien quotes: "It was through the medium of art therapy that I discovered the root of my illness, the change required to overcome anorexia, and a means of contacting my true self" (ibid. p.120).

Many practitioners use these methods today in addition to incorporating other creative media such as sand trays (where miniature objects and toys are placed to create stories and images which can then be utilised in a dialogue), psychodrama or dance/movement therapy and voice work. All of these methods can be effective. (See *On Becoming a Jungian Sandplay Therapist: The Healing Spirit of Sandplay in Nature and in Therapy* by Lenore F. Steinhardt. London and Philadelphia: Jessica Kingsley Publishers, 2013; www.psychodrama.org.uk/index.php; the Association for Dance Movement Psychotherapy UK at www.admt.org.uk/; and *The Singing Cure: Introduction to Voice Movement Therapy* by Paul Newham. London: Rider Books, 1993.)

SUMMARY

Through the use of Active Imagination, arts therapies and other creative modalities, Jung provides methods – as he himself used in *The Red Book* – for self-exploration as part of the journey of individuation.

CASE EXAMPLE

Perhaps the idea of progression via a path of individuation sounds like anathema to you. It is not a question of necessarily being unhappy with who one is, or where one is, in life. Although most of us could probably name aspects of life which could improve, is there not a need to grow and develop throughout life? The focus of our need will shift in line with the stage of life where we find ourselves, but most people do not wish to stagnate (except in periods of depression). In fact, depression may be an indicator that something is stuck and needs attention. While an in-depth exploration of depression is beyond the scope of this volume, a vignette from clinical work might help clarify this claim and elaborate how exploration can be transformative:

Luke presented for analysis with disrupted sleep patterns, sometimes associated with episodes of drug-taking. He thought he might be suffering with Seasonal Affective Disorder (SAD), which is when some people suffer as a result of less exposure to sunlight during winter. He had difficulty sustaining relationships with women and thought he might have traits associated with Asperger's Syndrome, which impairs the capacity to relate. Through our working together, this difficulty relating ameliorated to such an extent that he formed a family of his own which, although challenging, was clearly deeply sustaining. He also discovered he was profoundly affected by a birth trauma where both he and his mother almost died at his birth. This left an unconscious feeling of having almost killed his mother at birth, which manifested in depressive symptoms. When these matters became conscious, the affect associated with this trauma eased greatly and he was able to begin to let go of his sense of guilt.

SUMMARY

Outline:
We have a purposive function in life and can consciously work towards becoming more authentic. Individuation is the process by which we become separate psychological individuals, distinct from all others.

Gate diagram:
Jung created a diagram showing the different planes on which we can relate.

Stages of life:
Jung theorised the key stages of life as:

- Childhood

- Adolescence and early adulthood
- Adulthood and midlife
- Maturity and wisdom

Developmental model:
We looked at the contributions of Fordham, Klein, Winnicott and Bowlby.

Classical and Archetypal approaches:
These two approaches were reviewed.

Active Imagination and *The Red Book*:
Active Imagination is the method that Jung developed from his personal confrontation with the unconscious. He created a personal myth in *The Red Book*.

Mandalas:
Mandalas are an archetypal pattern which arise in all cultures the world over and which Jung saw as symbols of the Self.

Arts therapies:
The arts therapies (which include painting, sandplay, voice work, dramatherapy, psychodrama, dance/movement therapy) incorporate Jungian thinking and are used as methods for self-exploration as part of the journey of individuation.

Case example:
A clinical example was given to show how these methods may be helpful.

REFERENCES

Astor, J. (1995) *Michael Fordham: Innovations in Analytical Psychology.* Hove: Routledge.

Bowlby, J. (1969) *Attachment & Loss, Vol. 1. Attachment.* London: Hogarth Press and The Institute of Psycho-analysis.

Bowlby, J. (1973) *Attachment and Loss, Vol. 2. Separation: Anxiety and Anger.* London: Hogarth Press and The Institute of Psycho-analysis.

Bowlby, J. (1980) *Attachment and Loss, Vol. 3. Loss: Sadness and Depression.* London: Hogarth Press and The Institute of Psycho-analysis.

Bretton, A. (1924) Manifestoes of Surrealism. Ann Arbor, MI: University of Michigan Press, 1972.

Drob, S. (2012) *Reading The Red Book: An Interpretive Guide to C.G. Jung's Liber Novus*. New Orleans: Spring Journal Books.

Flournoy, T. (1900) *From India to the Planet Mars: A Case of Multiple Personality with Imaginary Languages* (Ed. S. Shamdasani; Trans. D. Vermilye). Princeton, NJ: Princeton University Press, 1994.

von Franz, M-L. (1964) "The Process of Individuation" in *Man and His Symbols* (Jung 1964). London: Picador, 1978.

Jaffé, A. (1963) *Memories, Dreams, Reflections*. London: Fontana Press.

Jung, C.G. (1913–30) (Ed. S. Shamdasani; Tr. M. Kyburz, J. Peck & S. Shamdasani). *The Red Book: Liber Novus*. London: W.W. Norton, 2009.

Jung, C.G. (1931) "The Stages of Life" in CW8.

Jung, C.G. (1939) "Conscious, Unconscious, and Individuation" in CW9i.

Jung, C.G. (1944) "The Conjunction" in CW14, 1963.

Jung, C.G. (1946) "Psychology of the Transference" in CW16.

Jung, C.G. (1950a) "A Study in the Process of Individuation" in CW9i.

Jung, C.G. (1950b) "Concerning Mandala Symbolism" in CW9i.

Jung, C.G. (1952) "Answer to Job" in CW11.

Jung, C.G. (1954) *Mysterium Coniunctionis*, CW14.

Jung, C.G. (1957) "Commentary on 'The Secret of the Golden Flower'" in CW13.

Jung, C.G. (1978) *Man and His Symbols*. London: Picador.

Jung, C.G. (1998) *Visions Seminars: Notes of the Seminar Given in 1930–34*. Vol. 2 (Ed. C. Douglas). London: Routledge & Princeton, NJ: Princeton University Press.

Kalsched, D. (1996) *The Inner World of Trauma: Archetypal Defences of the Personal Spirit*. London & New York: Routledge.

Newham, P. (1993) *The Singing Cure: Introduction to Voice Movement Therapy*. London: Rider Books.

Samuels, A. (1985) *Jung and the Post-Jungians*. London & New York: Routledge.

Samuels, A., Shorter, B. & Plaut, F. (1986) *A Critical Dictionary of Jungian Analysis*. London & New York: Routledge, 1997.

Schaverien, J. (1995) *Desire and the Female Therapist: Engendered Gazes in Psychotherapy and Art Therapy*. London & New York: Routledge.

Sedgwick, D. (2008) "Winnicott's Dream: Some Reflections on D.W. Winnicott and C.G. Jung" in *Journal of Analytical Psychology* Vol. 53 No. 4. pp. 543–560.

Shamdasani, Sonu (Ed.) (2009) C.G. Jung's *The Red Book: Liber Novus*. London: W.W. Norton & Company.

Steinhardt, L.F. (2013) *On Becoming a Jungian Sandplay Therapist: The Healing Spirit of Sandplay in Nature and in Therapy*. London & Philadelphia, PA: Jessica Kingsley Publishers.

BIBLIOGRAPHY

Stein, M. (1983, 2003) *In Midlife: A Jungian Perspective*. Putnam, CN.: Spring
    Publications.
Hillman, J. (1992) *The Myth of Analysis*. New York: Harper Perennial.
Henderson, J. (2005) *Thresholds of Initiation*. Wilmette, IL: Chiron Publications.

USEFUL WEBSITES

www.admt.org.uk/
https://aras.org/
http://thebowlbycentre.org.uk/
www.melanie-klein-trust.org.uk/home
www.psychodrama.org.uk/index.php

5

PSYCHOLOGICAL TYPES

OUTLINE

Jung worked on formulating his 'psychological types' from as early as 1913 and initially published these findings in German in 1921. This is one of his most unique contributions which has found its way into popular culture. Variations on his model are used especially in business settings to understand what might make people compatible in a working environment.

Jung's model introduces the terms introversion and extroversion – now in common parlance – which he described as attitudes. To attitudes, Jung added what he called the four functions (or modes of being/relating to the world): thinking, feeling, intuition, sensation (see Figure 5.1). While the first three of these are fairly self-explanatory, sensation is a rather ambiguous term which Jung uses to describe those who tend to use the five senses as a reality tester, or their mode of interacting with the world. Each of these functions can be experienced in an introverted or extraverted fashion. A further layer of nuance is added to denote whether one has a tendency to use these functions in a way that judges or simply perceives.

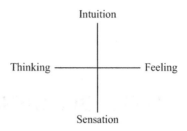

Figure 5.1   Basic model of psychological types

The model can be visualised with the aid of the diagram in Figure 5.1: Jungian analyst John Beebe in San Francisco describes Jung's model:

> This diagram can be read as a stick-figure representation of a right-handed person, who might be imagined standing erect with feet together and back placed flush against a blackboard with his or her arms spread-eagled, for the purpose of revealing the relations of his or her functions of consciousness. Each of the qualifying adjectives for the four functions shown... describes the "position" of one of the person's four functions of consciousness in relation to the others.
>
> (2004 p.91)

Putting intuition at the top in Figure 5.1 is random as there is no hierarchy to the order. Thinking and feeling are seen as a pair of opposites, as are sensation and intuition, so each pair would always be on a straight line opposite each other in this diagram whether vertically or horizontally.

Jung regards thinking and feeling as rational functions, which may sound counter-intuitive. What Jung means is that feeling is an evaluation of something. It helps if you distinguish feeling from sentiment since he is not talking about an emotion, but rather the function of feeling itself, a mode of assessing a situation:

> What I mean by feeling in contrast to thinking is a *judgment of value*: agreeable or disagreeable, good or bad... Feeling so defined is not an emotion or affect, which is... an involuntary manifestation. Feeling as I mean it is a judgment without any of the obvious bodily reactions that characterize an emotion. Like thinking, it is a *rational* function; whereas intuition, like sensation, is *irrational*. In so far as intuition is a "hunch" it is not a product of a voluntary act; it is rather an involuntary event.
>
> (Jung 1961 par. 502; emphasis in original)

Jung continues:

> These four functional types correspond to the obvious means by which
> consciousness obtains its orientation. *Sensation* (or sense perception)
> tells you that something exists; *thinking* tells you what it is; *feeling* tells
> you whether it is agreeable or not; and *intuition* tells you where it comes
> from and where it is going.
>
> (ibid. par. 503; emphasis in original)

Again, it may be hard to understand how sensation in particular can
be regarded as an irrational function, but what Jung means by this is
rather that it just *is*. As Canadian Jungian analyst Daryl Sharp explains:

> The term "irrational", as applied to the functions of sensation and
> intuition, does not mean illogical or unreasonable, but rather beyond
> or outside of reason. The physical perception of something does not
> depend on logic – things just *are*.
>
> (1987 p.17)

Jung makes it clear:

> all four functions should contribute equally: thinking should facilitate
> cognition and judgment, feeling should tell us how and to what extent
> a thing is important or unimportant for us, sensation should convey
> concrete reality to us through seeing, hearing tasting etc, and intuition
> should enable us to divine the hidden possibilities in the background,
> since these too belong to the complete picture of a given situation.
>
> (1923 par. 900)

Jung cautions against using these definitions too prescriptively. While
superficially they could be read like a sort of horoscope signifying
a general trend, his system is deceptively refined and accurate. Jung
even says that: "one can never give a description of a type, no matter
how complete, that would apply to more than one individual, despite the fact that in some ways it characterizes thousands of others"
(ibid. par. 895).

ANCIENT FOREBEARS

Hippocrates (fifth-century Greek physician regarded as the father
of Western medicine, who is still honoured today when qualifying
doctors swear a Hippocratic Oath) devised his own formulation. He
suggested that the human body was composed of four elements: air,

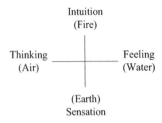

Figure 5.2   Jung's model incorporating Hippocrates' elements

water, fire and earth, which neatly correspond to Jung's types and can be transposed on to Jung's model as shown in Figure 5.2.

Take your time to get a sense in your body of how these ideas fit together: getting lost in thought can feel like being 'up in the air'; feelings can flow like water; dealing with the practical realities of life as indicated by the sensation type is like being 'down to earth', and intuition in turn can come in flashes like fire.

A desire to order thinking by devising models to categorise people is not new. Galen (c. 129 – c. 216/17 Common Era), a prominent Greek physician in the Roman Empire whose theories were to dominate Western medical thinking for centuries after his death, introduced terms with which you may be familiar to name what he called the 'four humours':

- *Melancholic* denotes a preponderance of black bile
- *Phlegmatic* a preponderance of phlegm or mucus (the Greek word *phlegma* means fire, with phlegm being regarded as the end-product of inflammation)
- *Sanguine* a preponderance of blood, and
- *Choleric* a preponderance of choler or yellow bile

(Jung 1936 par. 960)

It seems there may not be an exact correlation between the humours and Jung's model of psychological types, but it might be interesting to think about where they fit on the diagram in your own case.

As so often with Jung, one has to bear in mind his need to balance opposites. So we will see in the following how the different types balance each other in the psyche. To be fully one type would be too one-sided (and of course impossible); the other features of life would feel as if they were missing.

A further layer of complication is that we need to think about how the conscious attitude has its counter-balance in the unconscious (see Chapter 1).

GENERAL DESCRIPTION OF THE TYPES

The four types are seen as two sets of opposites. Thinking and feeling comprise one pair, and intuition and sensation another. Thinking and feeling are the ways we make a judgement about a situation, how we assess it. Sensation and intuition are how we perceive it. So Jung regards thinking and feeling as rational functions; sensation and intuition as irrational (or perhaps a-rational would be a better descriptor as he does not mean illogical but rather outside of reason). The overall influence of each function depends upon its relative position. Each function needs to be tempered by its opposite in the balance of the personality. *No type is better than any other.*

First, let us look at the characteristics of each type in turn, beginning with each function under the influence of extraversion followed by each function under the influence of introversion.

EXTRAVERSION

The extraverted attitude is directed to external objects. This implies one's orientation towards the world is generally outward, ie being engaged with external reality and being involved in life in a 'real world' sense, having relationships with people and finding the noise and busy-ness exciting and interesting. An extravert will enjoy parties and meetings and performing. They love the camera! They need to be among people and to express themselves. How extraversion tends to operate in conjunction with the functions looks something like this:

- **Thinking**

  Thinking does not imply intelligence in this context. It refers to the mode of facing and apprehending the world. The mind is instinctively the initial resource to be drawn on. They use thinking to work things out. The Extraverted Thinking type seeks objective reality in facts or ideas. In its negative form, this type may seem dull and banal or rigid. A positive form of this type might be a barrister or politician or flamboyant professor, all of whom need to 'think on their feet'. Someone with extraverted thinking will be able to extemporise and be confident their words flow easily; they can use their mind to win an argument without resorting to emotional tactics.

- **Feeling**

  Feeling here does not mean emotion. The Extraverted Feeling type will create a pleasant atmosphere at home. They are sociable, warm, outgoing. The feeling type leads with their feeling. They will 'feel out' a situation to take the emotional temperature in a room. While intuition senses the possibilities in the room, feeling senses the values or meaning. They are similar, but not the same. The feeling type is ruled more by heart than head. They will assess a situation predominantly by reference to feeling – does a situation feel right? This does not necessarily mean a person is good at handling their feelings, but rather they are the mode of experiencing the world. Indeed, when feeling is undeveloped it can be rather absolute and intractable. Someone of this type might become an actor or party host. They need to feel a rapport with others.

- **Sensation**

  Individuals who fall within this type tend to have a strong 'sense of reality' (if we can set aside philosophical arguments about the nature of reality for one moment!), which they treat as objective. Such rationality does not of course mean they are more immune than others to the vagaries of irrational fate. It relates rather to the attitude towards a situation and how it is dealt with. An Extraverted Sensation type is concerned with experiencing life in a direct way. This person will prize objective data – perhaps be a scientist or statistician. Anything ethereal is questioned. They seek interactions with the world which are physically exciting – orienteering, building, engaging with down-to-earth activities. They can read maps and lead you in the right direction when you get lost. They are inclined to be in touch with their senses (taste, touch, smell and so forth) as they experience life directly through them.

- **Intuition**
  Intuition is the sphere of the visionary who 'knows' without objective evidence. On a more ordinary scale, we all have intuition to some degree. Leaders in their field often intuit the direction which needs to be taken (although intuitives are notoriously lost when it comes to finding their way from A–B in a literal, physical sense. Do not ask an intuitive for directions on the street!). The intuitive thrives on the sphere of being an entrepreneur or speculator for instance, adventuring. They may be a good matchmaker, intuiting who would be good together. The gift of the Extraverted Intuitive is the ability to accurately imagine what happens next, but this can in the inferior function, Jung cautions, become paranoid thinking.

INTROVERSION

The introverted attitude is directed to interior subjective matters. This implies one's orientation towards life is generally inward, ie being introspective and content with one's own company, feeling fulfilled in a life of ideas and solitary in one's ways. The introvert may be solitary, being drawn to the interior life, but is not necessarily alone or lonely. How introversion tends to operate in conjunction with the functions might look something like this:

- **Thinking**
  The Introverted Thinking type is strongly influenced by ideas, especially those with a subjective foundation. Although this type may have a tremendous capacity to reason clearly, this may not necessarily translate into clarity in the outside world. Jung suggests, although this type may have knowledge to impart, he

does not make the best teacher as he is unconcerned with presentation (ie the outward reception of their ideas). The thinking type prizes rationality and leads by head before heart. The introverted thinking type might be a philosopher, or perhaps a fair boss who is able to consider matters coolly and rationally.

- **Feeling**
'Still waters run deep' characterises this type. Feelings are experienced deeply but without necessarily being apparent from the outside. For this reason paradoxically the Introverted Feeling type can appear rather cool, which is far from true. The focus tends to be inner and subjective and can become rather self-contained. This type might include religious folk whose focus is on silent (ie inner-directed) prayer. Feelings are the trait which actively guide such a type, in this case in an internally processed fashion so that from the outside they may seem quite mysterious. You might find yourself asking, what made them do/say that? They are reserved by nature. They might write poetry. In its negative form this type may become rather dominating and despotic, fomenting inner conflicts and creating dramas.

- **Sensation**
The Introverted Sensation type is concerned with objective reality. At least they are orientated not by any kind of rational judgement, but by the bare 'reality' of what is. This person is guided by the "intensity of the subjective sensation excited by the objective stimulus" (Jung 1921 par. 650). They like order. In the extreme, someone with this type can appear to be somewhat concrete or literal. Like each of the types, sensation needs to be balanced by its opposite – intuition. Introverted sensation is concerned with what goes on inside the body, watching how digestible things are, how calm or otherwise one's system feels in a given situation. They may appear to be disinterested, but internally they are taking in every detail of a situation. Sharp describes them as "like a highly sensitized photographic plate. The physical sensitivity to objects and other people takes in every smallest shade and detail – what they look like, how they feel to the touch, their taste and smell and the sounds they make" (1987 p.79). They would make a great witness in a trial.

- **Intuition**

  Intuition by its nature is experienced by reference to the internal realm and most particularly the unconscious. Intuition is usually perceived as imagery in 'the mind's eye' although not necessarily in a fully formed way. What makes intuition seem as if it comes from nowhere is how it can 'arrive' fully formed. It can feel as if someone who is highly intuitive can see right through you. The Introverted Intuitive tends to be highly imaginative and makes a great fiction writer, knowing what is in the zeitgeist. The introverted intuitive may pay little heed to their external appearance. Artists often fall within this category. In unfulfilled form, the person may seem like a crank, be chaotic and messy. This type can seem enigmatic and difficult to fathom.

THE PRINCIPAL AND AUXILIARY FUNCTIONS

The four functions are seen as having greater and lesser hold on us in terms of the order in which we identify with them, so that the function placed at the top of the diagram (Figure 5.3) (once we have established our type) is described as the superior function, the most influential in our make-up.

The remaining functions are seen in turn as the auxiliary function (on the left-hand side of the cross facing the page), the tertiary and the inferior functions. None of us is perfectly balanced between these four and it is a lifetime's struggle to develop the less-used functions. The auxiliary function's task in this schema is possible and useful in serving the dominant, superior function without making

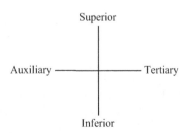

Figure 5.3   Principal and auxiliary functions

any claim to the autonomy of its own principle (1921 par. 668). Jung writes:

> [T]hinking as the primary function can readily pair with intuition as the auxiliary, or indeed equally well with sensation, but... never with feeling. Neither intuition nor sensation is antagonistic to thinking;... they are not of a nature equal and opposite to thinking, as feeling is – which, as a judging function, successfully competes with thinking – but are functions of perception, affording welcome assistance to thought.
>
> (ibid.)

> To be clear, Jung is not valuing thinking/feeling higher than intuition/ sensation, but rather emphasising the way these pairs are linked to each other. By their nature the two pairs of opposite functions (thinking/feeling and sensation/intuition) most naturally pair with a function from the other axis: one function from the vertical; one from the horizontal.

The inferior – fourth – function, being less developed, operates more slowly. Think of a person whose mind works like lightening for instance. This would indicate superior thinking. Sluggish thinking by the same token might be a sign it is an inferior function (by which of course no value judgement is intended). The inferior function is seen by Jung as the gateway to what he called the Shadow. This represents the characteristics we most wish *not* to identify with and are therefore the most difficult to access and acknowledge (see Chapters 2 and 3). Marie-Louise von Franz (1915–98), a collaborator and contemporary of Jung, put it like this:

> The inferior function is the door through which all the figures of the unconscious come into consciousness. Our conscious realm is like a room with four doors, and it is the fourth door by which the shadow... come[s] in. They do not enter as often through the other doors, which is in a way self-evident: the inferior function is so close to the unconscious and remains so barbaric and inferior and undeveloped that it is naturally the weak spot in consciousness through which the figures of the unconscious can break in.
>
> (2013 p.72)

> The two pairs (thinking/feeling and intuition/sensation) are always opposite one another by way of compensation or balance so, if your superior (ie strongest) function is feeling, thinking will be your inferior function and it needs most effort to use. In the same way, if intuition is your superior function, sensation will be your inferior function. It is probably self-explanatory: the auxiliary and tertiary functions in turn have successively less dominance in your overall personality. These opposites are always in tension and indeed need to be, like an ice-skater constantly adjusting her position to maintain balance and stay on her feet.

SUPERIOR FUNCTION

The most differentiated function (the superior function) tends to be the most conscious and therefore requires less explication. This is the function you will most likely identify with and be able to rely on. It is the mode of relating you most frequently use; the one which feels most natural to you.

INFERIOR FUNCTION

Inferior does not of course mean the same as negative in this context. Some people refer to particular feelings as having negative connotations. The author does not agree with such a formulation as, although some feelings are less pleasant to experience, there is often great meaning in them and in the long run they may be appreciated and valued. A quote from James Hillman (pioneer of Archetypal Psychology [1926–2011]) in his usual poetic style will help us to understand:

> Inferior feeling... may be characterised by contamination with the repressed, which tends to manifest, as the Scholastic would have said, in ira and cupiditas [anger and desire]. Inferior feeling is loaded with anger and rage and ambition and aggression as well as with greed and desire. Here we find ourselves with huge claims for love, with massive needs for recognition, and discover our feeling connection to life to be one of vast expectation composed of thousands of tiny angry resentments. This expectation has been called an omnipotent fantasy,

the expression of the abandoned child with his leftover feelings that
nobody wants to take care of.

(Hillman quoted in von Franz and Hillman 2013 pp.135–6)

Hillman goes on: "we [become] envious, jealous, depressed, feeding
on needs and their immediate gratification.... The cat neglected
becomes the unconscious tiger" (ibid. p.136).

UNCONSCIOUS ATTITUDE

At the risk of complicating matters, Jung saw the unconscious as
having its own *attitude* as a compensation for the conscious attitude
which serves as a balance. It can account for unfortunate 'slips'. An
example Jung gives is of an extroverted feeling type who usually has
excellent rapport with people, but can be rather tactless. These 'slips'
spring from the inferior half-conscious thinking (Jung 1921 par. 575).
(See Chapter 1 on the Unconscious).

Jung writes about an example which might help to clarify this:

> [a] lady who was proud of her intelligent understanding of psychology
> kept on dreaming about a certain woman whom she occasionally met in
> society. In real life she did not like her, thinking her vain, dishonest, and
> an intriguer. She wondered why she should dream of a person so unlike
> herself and yet, in the dream, so friendly and intimate, like a sister. The
> dream obviously wanted to convey the idea that she was "shadowed" by an
> unconscious character resembling that woman. As she had a very definite
> idea of herself, she was unaware of her own power-complex and her own
> shady motives, which had more than once led to disagreeable scenes that
> were always attributable to others but never to her own machinations.
>
> (1961 par. 508)

This might be seen in terms of what Jung called the Shadow (see
Chapter 3), but may also be thought about in terms of what psychological functions are embodied by the 'sister' figure in the dream, which
may help the dreamer identify what needs to be developed in themself.

PERSONAL TYPOLOGY

Inevitably, in thinking about a system of categories like this, we will
think about our own typology. It can be really quite difficult to work
out one's own type, not least of all because we are all always in the

process of 'becoming' (see Chapter 4 on Individuation), so our type is evolving as we develop and may even change over time. Some people know from an early age what career path they are drawn to for example; others take a lifetime to discover their potential, and some never do.

People often get stuck on how they can trust their intuition, and whether what they are experiencing is indeed intuition. You might find it interesting to experiment with noting down in a journal what you think might be an intuition to see if it can be trusted. (Genuine intuition is always spot on, but can be confused with fear, anxiety or paranoid thinking.)

One way to establish your own psychological type is to use the tool developed by Isabel Briggs Myers (1897–1980) and her mother Katharine Cook Briggs (1875–1968) called the Myers–Briggs Type Indicator®, which is used by many businesses and others to enable individuals to grow through an understanding and appreciation of individual differences and to enhance harmony and productivity in diverse groups. See www.myersbriggs.org/my-mbti-personality-type/, accessed 20 June 2015. (Please note that it does cost to do this test although it is possible you may find a free version.) It is important to realise that there is no 'good' or 'bad' type. They are all equal and indicate different propensities. The purpose of the tool is more to evaluate preferences or tendencies. It does not measure ability or character in a critical way. It is more helpful to think about the personality type as a way of understanding yourself and as a guide in thinking about how you make choices.

It is possible to dismiss Jung's theories of psychological types as a superficial schema which at first glance seems quite concrete and unsubtle. But, as with many of Jung's theories, it is possible to explore with increasing depth and to see them as much more complex and nuanced than at first glance. The types can be seen as a parlour game or like a horoscope, categorising things in quite generalised blocks of information applied to vast swathes of the population. It is also possible to get a more refined understanding of someone's psychological type in a very personal way. So for example, while the author is an Extraverted Feeling type, in fact she is an introvert but her feeling function is so prominent it becomes an extraverted function. Jung did not use this system to label people, but rather as a critical apparatus to sort and organise the welter of empirical data (Jung 1934 pp. xiv).

DISTORTED TYPE

One difficulty in ascertaining your own type can be if it has been distorted. This can happen if, when young, you are required to take on roles or characteristics in the family system which go against your natural grain. This happens in a subtle way. An example from clinical practice would be of a mature woman who had spent her life with a sense of something not being quite right, only to discover in her late 40s that she had been told a lie in early life. She had been told that she was not clever enough to go to grammar school to protect her sister who was not as bright. When she discovered this, it transformed her sense of self and she was able to develop her thinking function. She went on to achieve great success academically as a mature student. She found she had been squeezed into a shape that was not hers, and discovering this fact and the growth that was then possible, was deeply transformative. This distortion affected not only her thinking function. Her mother appeared to need her to be 'the efficient one' and so she was encouraged to develop her sensation function at the expense of her natural intuition. She felt quite skewed – or indeed skewered – by this dysfunctional twisting of her type. Analysis of these matters made a significant difference to the course of her life and enabled her to get on to her authentic path of individuation (see Chapter 4). The bald facts do not do justice to the deep, spiritual depths this realignment opened up, which allowed the woman to really become authentically herself. Her life was now back on its right track and she could begin to live more fully and be more fulfilled. She was able to access her thinking/feeling, intuition/sensation functions in a way that felt more natural to her and which makes life work more smoothly and feel more satisfying.

COUPLES

To add a further layer of complexity, you might notice that couples sometimes compensate for each other's opposite functions. An introverted person might feel quite happy with an extravert partner who embodies some of those qualities for the introvert. Or an intuitive might happily rely on a sensation type to give them some grounding in life. A feeling type will often marry a thinking type. Take a moment to think how this might apply to your own relationships.

FAIRY TALES

Classical Jungian analysts often use fairy tales and myths in analysis where archetypal patterns can be identified. It can be helpful to see that our own personal struggles often have a template in ancient antiquity where we can also see how the ancients resolved those struggles. Marie-Louise von Franz was the preeminent exponent of this method and published widely in this area. I will quote her at some length talking about the inferior function to give you a flavour:

> The behaviour of the inferior function is wonderfully mirrored in those fairy tales where there is the following structure: A king has three sons. He likes the two elder sons, but the youngest is regarded as a fool. The king then sets a task in which the sons may have to find the water of life, or the most beautiful bride.... Generally the two sons set out and get nowhere or get stuck, and then the third saddles his horse while everybody laughs and tells him he'd better stay at home by the stove where he belongs. But it is he who usually performs the great task. This fourth function – the third son, but the fourth figure in the setup – has, according to the myths, different superficial qualities. Sometimes he is the youngest, sometimes he is a bit idiotic, and sometimes he is a complete fool.
>
> (2013 p.15)

She goes on:

> [t]he fool is an archetypal religious figure, embracing more than only the inferior function. He implies a part of the human personality, or even of humanity, which remained behind and therefore still has the original wholeness of nature.... In mythology, as soon as the fool appears as the fourth in a group of four people, we have a certain right to assume that he mirrors the general behaviour of an inferior function.
>
> (ibid.)

Take a moment to think about 'fools' you have encountered and how they often make a fool of us by actually being quite clever. Many comedians work on this very premise. The 'Fool' is seen as an archetype in all its various cultural disguises. Think of the Fool in Shakespeare's King Lear, or Baldrick in the BBC's *Blackadder* series (Curtis & Elton 1983–89). A question (not intended as a trick!): was Baldrick a Fool or Idiot? What are the differences?

JOHN BEEBE'S EIGHT-FUNCTION MODEL

Jungian analyst John Beebe has developed an eight-function model of psychological types based on Jung's original schema, which can usefully be applied in particular to dream analysis. It suggests we think about each character in the dream as representing different aspects of our psychological type. It is a complex model to describe. As you will have seen above, Jung's model postulated four functions (thinking, feeling, sensation and intuition), each influenced by whether we are predominantly introverted or extraverted. These are balanced in one direction or another with the most dominant function termed the superior function. This is counterbalanced by an inferior function and so forth (see Figure 5.3).

Beebe's eight-function model introduces a whole opposing personality (which he introduces by using the archetypes such as hero and anima or animus for example) representing a further four positions, which takes us into ever more subtle analysis of the individual and extends Jung's thinking. Beebe postulates what is missing in a dream by tracking which functions and attitudes are present and in what position. This then helps the dreamer see what needs to be developed or needs attention.

He associates each psychological type with archetypes, which he diagrams as shown in Figure 5.4 using his own personality type for illustrative purposes.

An example of how this model is valuable in clinical practice can be seen from the following dream from the author's practice:

> I was getting onto a train, which was an old-fashioned slow "chug chug" train. I was with an auntie [although not the real one]. There was also a girl who was in fact only a couple of years younger than me. There were some other people in the carriage, which was very homely and it was as if they were sitting on sofas facing each other. The three of them seemed to be in one section. Then behind me was a big man with a smart white shirt who was faceless. They had been downstairs earlier, which looked like a big ticket office area. The station was downstairs and you had to go up to the platforms.

Initially it had sounded as if the three of them formed the party, but then the fourth person, the faceless man, was mentioned. (The number four is seen as significant in Jungian psychology as it represents

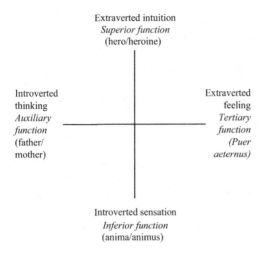

Figure 5.4 John Beebe's eight-function model

wholeness. This idea partly relates to the wholeness of Jung's four-function model of psychological types we have been discussing.) There were vague other people who all seemed to be part of the group travelling together. When the dreamer mentioned the man/fourth person, this brought to mind the idea of typology and the idea about whether the man represented this dreamer's fourth function (or Shadow). Thinking about the dream in terms of John Beebe's functional model in which all the characters in the dream represent different aspects, this dreamer would be the Hero/ego of the dream; the auntie would be the mother; the girl the anima. The faceless man (who we suggested was the dreamer's potential) might represent the Shadow. The dreamer woke with a good feeling from this dream. Since the dream had been cut off by the alarm clock, I encouraged him to 'dream the dream onwards' (ie using Active Imagination – referred to in Chapter 4 on Individuation – to amplify the image to help us gain even greater meaning from the dream) by asking where the train might have been going. This drew a blank but he thought the station was Paddington, his favourite station. It heads west. What might that mean? He had recently spent a fulfilling weekend in the West Country. This imagery evoked ideas of sunset and death.

Inevitably the dream could have been unpacked further and further to imagine what was missing and so on. There is no complete interpretation of a dream but this is offered as an example of how these ideas can be used in practice.

Next time you dream, you might experiment with unpacking it along these lines and see if you find that helpful or interesting.

DRAWING TOGETHER

If we bring the different models together, this gives us a good foundation on which to think about how these various layers relate to one another and which hopefully in turn facilitate us to understand how we function in relation to others and their sometimes vastly different 'type' character structures (see Figure 5.5).

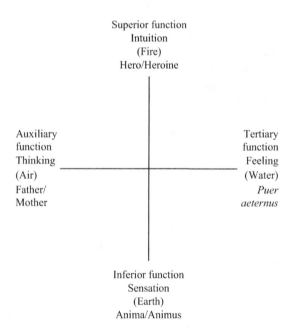

Superior function
Intuition
(Fire)
Hero/Heroine

Auxiliary function Thinking (Air) Father/ Mother

Tertiary function Feeling (Water) *Puer aeternus*

Inferior function
Sensation
(Earth)
Anima/Animus

Figure 5.5 Combined model

I would reiterate that the functions could appear in any of the four positions and the archetypal character associated with each would vary for every individual.

Using your imagination, perhaps with the help of a Myers-Briggs test, how do you see your own set of types?

In the next chapter we will see how these ideas can be further applied to dreams.

SUMMARY

We have seen in this chapter how Jung categorised his Psychological Types into two attitudes of introversion and extraversion and four functions: thinking, feeling, intuition and sensation. These are seen as the most prominent being the superior function, the next most prominent being the auxiliary function, followed by tertiary and inferior functions. The inferior function is seen as the gateway to the Shadow, which represents the characteristics with which we most wish *not* to identify.

We have looked at how the unconscious attitude can compensate the conscious: at personal typology, distorted types, and the way in which opposites can attract in couples. I reviewed how types can be applied to fairy tales and myth.

John Beebe's eight-function model has been included to show greater levels of subtlety in how these models can be used, particularly in dream interpretation.

A clinical example was discussed before combining the models to see how they fit together.

REFERENCES

Beebe, J. (2004) "Understanding Consciousness through the Theory of Psychological Types" in *Analytical Psychology: Contemporary Perspectives in Jungian Analysis* (Ed. J. Cambray & L. Carter). Hove: Brunner-Routledge. pp.83–115.

Curtis, R & Elton, B. (1983–89) *Blackadder*. BBC TV.

Jung, C.G. (1921) "General Description of the Types" in CW6.

Jung, C.G. (1923) "Psychological Types" in CW6.

Jung, C.G. (1934) "Foreword to the Argentine Edition" in CW6.

Jung, C.G. (1936) "Psychological Typology" in CW6.

Jung, C.G. (1961) "The Problem of Types in Dream Interpretation" in CW 18.

Hillman, J. (2013) "The Feeling Function" in von Franz & Hillman, 2013. pp.95–178.

Sharp, D. (1987) *Psychological Types: Jung's Model of Typology.* Toronto: Inner City Books.

von Franz, M. (2013) *Lectures on Jung's Typology.* (von Franz and Hillman) Putnam, CN: Spring Publications.

BIBLIOGRAPHY

Giannini, J.L. (2004) *Compass of the Soul: Archetypal Guides to a Fuller Life.* Gainsville, FL: Center for Applications of Psychological Types.

USEFUL WEBSITES

The Myers-Briggs Foundation:

www.myersbriggs.org/my-mbti-personality-type/mbti-basics/the-16-mbti-types.htm

Type Resources: www.type-resources.com/index.html

The Center for Applications of Psychological Types: www.capt.org/home.htm?bhcp=1

6

DREAMS

"Who looks outside dreams; who looks inside awakes."

C.G. Jung (1916)

Have you ever awoken from a dream and not known whether you were awake or asleep? Sometimes it takes a moment to work out whether the dream was the 'reality' and whether you really are now awake. Dreams exert a fascinating power over us that create a kind of wonder.

STRUCTURE

Dreams often follow a dramatic structure:

1. Setting (place, protagonists, time, scene)
2. Development of plot
3. Culmination – turning point/change
4. Solution/cleansing/relief/result

Broadly this follows Aristotle's template for action in the *Poetics* (c. 330 BCE, the earliest surviving work of dramatic theory), applied by Jung to dreams:

- Exposition (the setting forth of the detail)
- Peripeteia (a Greek word meaning the turn of fortunes dramatised in the dream – or life)
- Crisis (in the sense of a sense of suspense indicating a turning point, perhaps a decision)
- Lysis (final unravelling or denouement)

(1948a pars. 561–4)

This is a classical or archetypal structure of stories or dreams.

Jung sees dreams as guiding the dreamer, revealing situations symbolically as follows:

> The whole dream-work is essentially subjective, and a dream is a theatre in which the dreamer is himself the scene, the player, the prompter, the producer, the author, the public and the critic.
>
> (1948b par. 509)

For Jung the dream can be seen in the following ways:

- The dream is the unconscious response to a conscious situation.
- (This may be a compensatory attitude which can help to counter a conscious one.)
- The dream arises from conflict between conscious and unconscious.
- The unconscious is hinting at a possible change of conscious attitude.
- The unconscious is depicted in a pure form in a way which can feel quite overwhelming and oracular.
- The dream is a way of communicating with the unconscious; not an attempt to conceal true feelings.
- Symbols are seen as a guide to help the dreamer.

The oldest recorded dream is in *The Epic of Gilgamesh* (A. George trans. London: Penguin Classics, 2000) written in ancient Mesopotamia 1,000 years before the Bible. (Mesopotamia is the area of the rivers Tigris and Euphrates corresponding to modern-day Iraq, Kuwait, the north-eastern section of Syria, south-eastern Turkey and smaller parts of south-western Iran).

In the epic, Gilgamesh and Enkidu (the two main characters) both have dreams that act as messages which seem prophetic. They come to value them and see dreams as messages from the gods. The first dream depicts Enkidu's arrival on earth as a meteorite. It is so weighty that Gilgamesh is unable to move it but he manages to do so with assistance. He takes the meteorite to his mother's house and she accurately foretells that Enkidu will save Gilgamesh's life (Tablet 1 line 268).

The dream reads:

> The stars of the heavens appeared above me,
> like a rock from the sky one fell down before me.
> I lifted it up, but it weighed too much for me,
> I tried to roll it, but I could not dislodge it.
> The land or Uruk [of which Gilgamesh is King] was standing around it,
> the land was gathered about it.
> A crowd was milling about before it,
> the menfolk were thronging around it.
> Like a babe-in-arms they were kissing its feet,
> like a wife I loved it, caressed and embraced it.
> I lifted it up, set it down at your feet,
> and you, O mother, you made it my equal.
>
> (Tablet 1 lines 247–58)

We are told Gilgamesh invokes the dream by making an offering to the gods and creating the conditions to have a dream.

We can follow his example. We will look at how we can encourage dreams ourselves by recording them. Even at times when a dream seems powerful and unforgettable, they tend to slip away if an effort is not made to capture them. A useful method is to keep a pen and paper by the side of the bed, or alternatively a voice-recording device which can be found on smart phones nowadays. Everybody dreams – even if you are not aware of this. Perhaps you might experiment with finding out by keeping a watchful ear/eye out and noting them down. It can be helpful not only to note down the narrative, but to draw the dream too. (You don't have to be an artist to try this. The purpose is not to create an aesthetic object for display, but is more about capturing a feeling and an image; finding ways to increase your awareness of what is contained in the dream to facilitate your understanding of the meaning or indeed meanings as dreams can have significance on many different levels simultaneously.) Note also the feeling(s) in the dream and as you awaken. These form a vital aspect of the dream itself and will help you make sense of them. How did you feel in the dream? How did you feel on waking? "Stick to the image" was the injunction of James Hillman (1926–2011), who studied with Jung in the 1950s and went on to establish Archetypal Psychology, an offshoot of Jungian Analytical Psychology. The context and timing of the dream are also highly significant, so note them too.

INCUBATION

In ancient antiquity Asclepius, a pre-Greek god associated with medicine and healing (usually seen depicted with a serpent entwined around his staff), was regarded as an oracle. Asclepius (whose father in ancient myth was Apollo) practised dream incubation as a method of healing at his temple in Epidaurus. The person seeking his guidance had to take a ritual bath before entering the sanctuary to cleanse both body and soul. The person consulting Asclepius would sleep on a couch (which has its modern equivalent in the analytic couch used by psychoanalysts) in the sanctuary. There were statues in the sanctuary of the god of sleep (Hypnos) and the god of dreams (Oneiros) to invoke their presence. Dreams were not interpreted. They simply did their work of healing (see Meier 1989 pp.49–60). Perhaps you might try calling up a dream of your own if you have a problem to solve. This cannot of course be done in a controlling way; a certain humility is required to approach the gods!

FREUD

Sigmund Freud's *The Interpretation of Dreams* (1953), one of the most significant books of the 20th century, represents the beginning of psychoanalysis. Freud called dreams the 'Royal road' to the discovery of the unconscious. Freud's theory outlined in *The Interpretation of Dreams* is that dreams represent wish-fulfilment (albeit sometimes disguised, repressed or infantile). His interpretative method involves thinking about dreams via condensation (by which he means that dream elements – themes, images, figures, ideas etc – combine so that the dream compacts or condenses the elements) and displacement (a situation is transferred to another, usually making it more palatable to grasp what is being suggested by the dream). Freud sees the mind as an essentially divided entity, with an unconscious lurking to catch you. For Freud the mind might be characterised as being grubby or repressed, highlighting dramatic memories and drives of sex and aggression which have to be dealt with.

While Freud thinks about dreams as being symbolic, he is using this word in a way that is less nuanced than it becomes for Jung (whose ideas on dreams we will come to shortly). For Freud the meaning of a dream-element is more fixed (and this applies not only to dreams but in art, literature, and culture). Freud maintains that the great majority of symbols in dreams are sexual, and he lists copious examples which can be used to represent copulation, other sexual acts and the genital organs of both sexes. See Freud's essay "Symbolism in Dreams" for more examples (*The Standard Edition of the Complete Psychological Works of Sigmund Freud* [Tr. J. Strachey] Vol. 15. London: Hogarth Press, 1963, pp.149–69).

It is well known that the body can be the spur to a dream, so that, if your bladder is bursting during the night, it is common to dream of needing to go to the toilet.

Sometimes there is an external stimulus. In *The Interpretation of Dreams* Freud cites a famous dream by Cardinal Jean-Sifrein Maury (1746–1817) dreamt while he was lying in bed ill:

> *it was during the... [the French Revolution]. After witnessing a number of frightful scenes of murder, he was finally... brought before the revolutionary tribunal. There he saw Robespierre, Marat, Fouquier-Tinville, and the rest of the grim heroes of those terrible days. He was questioned..., and... was condemned, and led to the place of execution surrounded by an immense mob. He climbed on to the scaffold and was bound to the plank by the executioner. It was tipped up. The blade of the guillotine fell. He felt his head being separated from his body, woke up in extreme anxiety – and found that the top of the bed had fallen down, and had struck his cervical vertebrae just in the way in which the blade of the guillotine would actually have struck them.*

(1953 pp.26–7)

JUNG

Jung saw the mind as being teleological (that is, "having an orientation to ends or purposes rather than causes" [Samuels *et al* 1986 p.148]). Jung has a perhaps more positive outlook although certainly not lacking in grit. See for instance his formulation of *The Shadow*, which is an aspect we all contain representing our more reprehensible facets or "the thing [a person] has no wish to be" (1946 par. 470) (Chapter 3). For Jung the mind is essentially the seat of creativity.

The dream is not seen as a disguised attempt to hide things. By working things through in dreams, we work towards greater wholeness as individuals and thus healing (see Chapter 4 on Individuation). They are a creative source which helps you live your life to the fullest extent.

Contemporary Jungian analyst Jean Knox in London introduces an important new approach to dream work which is evolving as discoveries are made in neuroscience for instance and other fields of research:

> More recently, an attachment/trauma perspective has highlighted the destructive effects of unprocessed trauma on the symbolic functioning of the human psyche. This approach suggests that dreams may sometimes provide powerful images that reflect dissociated aspects of the human psyche and sense of self, with its accompanying emotional state and psychic defences.
>
> (Knox see https://childpsychotherapy.org.uk/civicrm/event/ info?id=77&reset=1, accessed 8 August 2016)

In interpreting dreams, Jung devised a method he called 'amplification', which was an expansion of Freud's method of 'free association' in that he would think not only about the images which came directly to mind, but make links to their comparative mythological and historical roots to glean deeper insight. It can be quite astonishing to find that a situation we have experienced has a template in antiquity. While this can inspire the notion that these things can be survived, we have of course to discover our own unique ways of approaching these problems. Does this give you a sense of feeling connected to the past? Perhaps hope for the future?

Jung saw dream images as being symbolic, which he described as:

> an expression of an intuitive idea that cannot yet be formulated in any other or better way... [They are] attempts to express something for which no verbal concept yet exists.
>
> (1931 par. 105)

Jung distinguishes symbols from signs and semiotics, which have more concrete meanings. A signpost giving directions is a sign. Semiotics designates a direction by for instance allegory or metaphor. A symbol has a complex bundle of meanings rolled into one so that it may contain literal, metaphorical, unconscious meaning to a dreamer (in this case), which could not be expressed in a more precise or economical way. The symbol may well contain highly personalised information specific to the individual although drawing on an archetypal pattern. This gives the symbol a numinous quality. So a dream might contain an image of, say, an owl. That owl seen by someone else might appear to be simply an owl. To the dreamer it may carry unique associations related to what owls mean to the individual, when the dreamer may have seen such a creature perhaps, the specific breed, the feeling tone associated with the image in the dream and multiple other factors. All will contribute to the overall quality of experience, which would turn this otherwise innocuous image into what Jung would refer to as a living symbol.

Jung was critical of Freud's free association method as he observed that free association to any image would produce the same results (1961a par. 425) and lead us to the core of a complex without the psyche needing to produce a dream.

Jung saw dreams as a deep and meaningful product of the mind, which he treasured. In his *Red Book* (see Chapter 4) Jung noted:

> I must learn that the dregs of my thought, my dreams, are the speech of my soul. I must carry them in my heart, and go back and forth over them in my mind, like the words of the person dearest to me. They are the guiding words of the soul.
>
> (Shamdasani (Ed.) 2009 p.233)

Ultimately, the breakdown of the relationship between Jung and Freud (see Preface) and the differences between them came to a head through a dream Jung had (mentioned in Chapter 1). He dreamt he was in his house, apparently on the first floor, in a cosy, pleasant drawing-room furnished in the style of the eighteenth century [as was his actual home growing up]. He went down to the ground floor (which he had never seen before), and discovered it was furnished in the style of the sixteenth century. He went further down to the cellar which was old Roman in style. He lifted a stone slab to find a narrow flight of stairs leading down to a cave which he saw was obviously a prehistoric tomb containing two skulls, some bones and broken shards of pottery.

For a full version of the dream, see 1961b par. 484 or *Memories, Dreams, Reflections* (Jaffé 1963 p.182). The dream was significant to Jung in two important ways: the timeline in the dream travelling further and further back galvanised Jung's thinking about the nature of the Collective Unconscious (see Chapter 1), which was pivotal Stet pivotal in formulating his independent ideas. Secondly, Jung sadly felt compelled to pander to Freud's way of thinking by interpreting the dream along the lines of wish-fulfilment. He reported that he thought the skulls might refer to members of Jung's own family whose death he might desire, which satisfied Freud but not Jung who knew he had dissembled. This was clearly an untenable situation which had to end, so this was a momentous moment.

FAMOUS DREAMS

Paul McCartney has spoken about how the melody of The Beatles' song "Yesterday" came to him in a dream. He was staying in a small attic room in London in 1965, while the band was filming Help! He woke up with a tune in his head, he said, and immediately decided to play it. He describes getting out of bed and sitting at the piano when his hands automatically found: "G, found F sharp minor 7th – and that leads you through then to B to E minor, and finally back to E. I liked the melody a lot." He struggled to even believe he had written it himself since it arose in a dream. Then he thought: "'No, I've never written anything like this before.' But I had the tune, which was the most magic thing!" (http://news.bbc.co.uk/1/hi/magazine/8092029.stm, accessed 29 May 2015).

In the summer of 1816, Mary Wollstonecraft Godwin, and her lover Percy Shelley, visited the poet Lord Byron at his villa near Lake Geneva in Switzerland. Wollstonecraft Godwin, later Mary Shelley through marriage, has described how her famous work *Frankenstein* was inspired by a waking dream she had that night in Byron's villa. She describes how with closed eyes she envisioned in her mind's eye:

> the pale student of unhallowed arts kneeling beside the thing he had put together. I saw the hideous phantasm of a man stretched out, and

then, on the working of some powerful engine, show signs of life, and
stir with an uneasy, half-vital motion.

> (http://news.bbc.co.uk/1/hi/magazine/8092029.stm, accessed 29
> May 2015)

Golfer Jack Nicklaus reports a dream he had about his golf swing:

all at once I realized I wasn't holding the club the way I've... been
holding it lately. I've been having trouble collapsing my right arm
taking the club head away from the ball, but I was doing it perfectly in
my sleep.

> (http://news.bbc.co.uk/1/hi/magazine/8092029.stm,
> accessed 29 May 2015)

When he went to the course the following day, he tried it the way he
had dreamt it, and it worked!

Organic chemist Friedrich August Kekulé von Stradonitz (1829–
96) had a dream that helped him discover the benzene molecule and
structure. In a talk in his honour, Kekulé recounted the following
dreams:

I fell into a reverie, and lo, the atoms were gamboling before my eyes!
Whenever, hitherto, these diminutive beings had appeared to me,
they had always been in motion; but up to that time, I had never been
able to discern the nature of their motion. Now, however, I saw how,
frequently, two smaller atoms united to form a pair; how a larger one
embraced the two smaller ones; how still larger ones kept hold of three
or even four of the smaller; whilst the whole kept whirling in a giddy
dance. I saw how the larger ones formed a chain, dragging the smaller
ones after them, but only at the ends of the chain.

Some years later, the more famous incident occurred, a dream in
which Kekulé realised that the benzene molecule had a circular
structure:

I was sitting writing on my textbook, but the work did not progress;
my thoughts were elsewhere. I turned my chair to the fire and dozed.
Again the atoms were gamboling before my eyes. This time the smaller
groups kept modestly in the background. My mental eye, rendered
more acute by the repeated visions of the kind, could now distinguish
larger structures of manifold conformation; long rows sometimes more
closely fitted together all twining and twisting in snake-like motion.
But look! What was that? One of the snakes had seized hold of its own
tail, and the form whirled mockingly before my eyes. As if by a flash

of lightning I awoke; and this time also I spent the rest of the night in working out the consequences of the hypothesis.

(Benfey *Journal of Chemical Education*, Vol. 35, 1958, p.21
quoted in Roberts 1989 p.77)

Albert Einstein (1879–1955) is said to have dreamt about sledding with friends one night. We are told he started to slide down the hill only to find his sled was going faster and faster until he realised he was approaching the speed of light. It says he looked up at that point and saw the stars. They were being refracted into colours he had never seen before. We are told he was filled with a sense of awe, which gave him a feeling that he was looking at something which encapsulated the most important meaning in his life. At the end of his life, Einstein said he knew he had to understand that dream and considered that his entire scientific career was a meditation on that dream.

TYPES OF DREAMS

You will likely have noticed that there are different types of dreams:

Traumatic dreams/nightmares: Probably we are all familiar with the sensation of waking from a dream that has such a powerful negative grip on us that we call it a nightmare. It can stay with the dreamer for many hours or even years. It might contain frightening or grotesque creatures/characters, or familiar figures in frightening or unfamiliar form. A nightmare usually leaves us shaking with fear and feeling quite discombobulated.

Day residue/'trivial' dreams: Although some dreams can appear to be quite superficial and be a way of sifting recent events from the day before which might unconsciously be preying on your mind (see Chapter 1 on The Unconscious), much can be gleaned from exploring these. Clinically people often come in saying they "only remember a snippet" of dream, which can often elicit deep and significant material.

Anxious dreams: Dreaming can be a way of ameliorating anxiety. Anxiety can get stuck in the body as energy and even become illness. Dreaming is one way in which the organism rebalances and reboots the system.

Punning dreams: These are often really witty. They play with the idea that words sometimes have multiple meanings or indeed that they sound like words with altogether different meanings. Anthony Stevens (1995) cites an example from antiquity in which he tells us that to dream of uncovering one's behind means one is about to lose one's parents, which makes no sense at all until you discover that the Egyptian word for buttocks closely resembled the word for orphan.

Recurring dreams: Often vary in some detail but recapitulate the same territory in different ways, looking at issues from different perspectives, refracted through different lenses. They are a way of working through a dilemma and seem to stop when the issue is resolved. They can recur over many years. If a dream does keep recurring, you better listen! Something significant is being communicated. They can refer to both past events and future. Jung cites a recurring dream of his own in which he discovered a part of a wing of his house which he did not know about:

> Sometimes it was the place where my parents lived – who had died long ago – where my father, to my great surprise, had a laboratory in which he studied the comparative anatomy of fishes, and where my mother ran a hostelry for ghostly visitors. Usually the wing or independent guest-house was an historical building several hundred years old, long forgotten, yet my ancestral property. It contained interesting old furniture and towards the end of this series... I discovered an old library whose books were unknown to me. Finally, in the last dream, I opened one of the old volumes and found in it a profusion of the most marvellous symbolic pictures. When I awoke, my heart was pounding with excitement.
>
> (1961b par. 478)

Shortly after this dream a parcel arrived containing a 16th-century alchemical volume with many fascinating symbolic pictures, which instantly reminded Jung of the library in the dream. Since the rediscovery of alchemy forms an important part of Jung's life as a pioneer of psychology (see Chapter 7 on Alchemy), the motif of the unknown annex of his house can be understood as an anticipation of a new field of interest and research for Jung which may have been just bubbling underneath the surface at the time of the dream, perhaps in an unformed way that he had not yet fully identified.

Transference dreams: A term used in the clinical setting to denote dreams which relate to the relationship between analyst and patient (or the terms analysand or client are sometimes used). These are often the source of deeply significant information which can then be worked on together and can prove to be pivotal.

Lucid dreams: These are dreams where people believe they are awake in the dream and able to make 'conscious' choices about the trajectory of the dream. The author regards these with some scepticism. The idea may derive from an overly developed need to control matters in life.

Shared dreams: Couples sometimes report having had the same dream. These likely occur more frequently than we realise but we only find out when we share our dreams with others. Similarly, Jung talks of a colleague who noted down all the dreams which arose in his house. He lived with a wife, two children and a maid. He noted their dreams as well as those of his patients and was astonished to find that his patients' problems would appear in the dreams of his maid, his wife and his children (1938 pp. 14–15)! As Shakespeare had it: "There are more things in heaven and earth, Horatio, Than are dreamt of in your philosophy" (Hamlet Act 1, Scene 5, lines 168–9, William Shakespeare).

Pre-cognitive dreams: There are many examples of these. In the wake of the 11 September 2001 attacks many people reported remarkable examples which you will find with an online search. I cite this example because many spoke about their dreams following 11 September and so they came into the public realm.

Jung quotes an example told to him by a friend at university whose father had promised the boy a trip to Spain if he did well in an exam. Prior to the exam he had the following dream:

> *He is in a Spanish town and follows a street to a square into which several streets lead, and which is defined by a cathedral. He strolls across the square and turns right, as he first wants to have a look at the cathedral from the side. As he is turning into that street, a carriage with two Isabella horses is coming.*

(1938 p.11)

The dream made such an impression on the boy because the image was of such great beauty and brilliance. Three weeks later, after the exam, the boy travelled to Spain. From there Jung reports he received the news that the dream had come true. In a Spanish town he came to such a square. At once he remembered the dream, and said to himself: "Now, if the horses in the side street also came true!" He went into the side street – and the horses were there! (1938 p.11).

Warning dreams: These partly fall within the category of precognitive. An example cited by Jung: "Another child dreams that the mother wants to kill herself. Crying, the child runs into the room of the mother, who is already awake; she is just on the point of committing suicide" (1938 p.13).

Jung cites a further example in explicating that dreams are sometimes compensatory so that dreaming of vertiginous drops, balloons, flying and falling are sometimes related to an over-estimation of oneself, unrealistic opinions or grandiose fantasies. Jung:

> If the warning of the dream is not heeded, real accidents take its place... I remember the case of a man who was inextricably involved in a number of shady affairs. He developed an almost morbid passion for dangerous mountain-climbing as a sort of compensation: he was trying to "get above himself". In one dream he saw himself stepping off the summit of a high mountain into the air. When he told me his dream, I instantly saw the risk he was running, and I tried my best to emphasise the warning and convince him of the need to restrain himself. I even told him that the dream meant his death in a mountain accident. It was in vain. Six months later he "stepped off into the air". A mountain guide watched him and a young friend letting themselves down on a rope in a difficult place... both went down and were killed.

(1961b par. 471)

Of course, most dreams cannot be read so literally. This reading relies on Jung's highly developed intuitive function (see Chapter 5 on Psychological Types).

Problem–solving dreams: Help the dreamer to deal with issues. (See also *dream incubation* below.) They may even offer a solution to a problem playing on one's mind.

'Big' dreams: These are so powerful that they often remain in the mind over years as being significant. These dreams can feel as if they are 'sent by God', if you have such a belief. They can be a defining moment in time and remain vivid in the mind's eye.

Social/collective dreams: An example would be Jung's famous dream vision, which you will find in *Memories, Dreams, Reflections* (Jaffé 1963). In October 1913 he was gripped with the image of a:

> monstrous flood covering all the northern and low-lying lands between the North Sea and the Alps. When it came up to Switzerland I saw that the mountains grew higher to protect our country. I realised that a frightful catastrophe was in progress. I saw the mighty yellow waves, the floating rubble of civilisation, and the drowned bodies of uncounted thousands. Then the whole sea turned to blood.
>
> (1963 p.199)

Two weeks later he had the same vision more powerfully followed by further dreams in a similar vein which, in retrospect, he saw as pre-figuring the coming World War which began on 1 August 1914. So this could also be regarded as pre-cognitive.

Most of these categories are self-explanatory.

DREAM SERIES

Once you track dreams you begin to notice there are times when a narrative is carried forward from one to another. Jung used dream series as a kind of research tool or 'control test':

> In dream series, the dreams are connected to one another in a meaningful way, as if they tried to give expression to a central content from ever-varying angles.
>
> (Jung 1938 p.3)

Chronology is not necessarily linear in dreams so order may seem jumbled. Rather, Jung sees the strands as emanating from a central core of consciousness, or centre of meaning (1938 p.10).

A recent example (of a series of two connected sets of images) would be a dream the author recently came across of *a woman having a broken front left tooth which was hanging precariously*. A few days later the woman dreamt *of a butterfly flapping in her face, which came to land on the left-hand side of her face just near the position of the tooth in the previous dream*. The left-hand side is often associated with the unconscious (see Chapter 1), so the dream could be interpreted as meaning that there is something fragile in the unconscious which needs attention. (I would emphasise that meaning is gleaned via multiple factors such as the feeling on waking, the timing, context and personal as well as collective associations.)

British psychoanalyst Charles Rycroft (1914–98) recounts a terrific example of the progression that can be found in a dream series when he cites a man who:

> dreamt successively that he was approaching his father's house, that he had entered it, that he was in his father's study which was occupied by someone else, that he found a room which he at first thought was his own but turned out to be his brother's, and finally that he found a room in his father's house which was his own.

(1979 p.127)

You might readily imagine how significant that must have felt to the dreamer to have worked through these stages to find himself metaphorically finding a sense of belonging in his father's house. This conveys to the boy a feeling that he is in his father's heart, or that he had found his place in life.

EXPLORING DREAMS

A useful way of trying to elicit meaning from dreams is to dialogue with dream images. Jung was an artist himself and used various artistic media in his personal explorations. He experimented with his own dreams by writing them down in notebooks, which he then transcribed and embellished with paintings in what became *The Red Book* (2009). He would steep himself in these characters and allow his imagination to lead him (see Chapter 4 on Individuation).

From these explorations he developed a method which he came to call *Active Imagination*, whereby he encouraged dialogue between unseen parts of the personality as they manifest in a dream for example – a method which has been influential on contemporary humanistic and arts psychotherapists including in particular Gestalt Therapy (pioneered by Fritz Perls [1893–1970]). See *Self & Society* Vol. 43 Issue 3, which contains the proceedings of a conference exploring the links between Analytical Psychology and the various humanistic psychotherapies in contemporary practice (Williams (Ed.) 2015).

Exploring dreams using these methods can be done privately or with others. Working with an analyst is the method *par excellence* but this may not be possible. You might want to explore them in solitude, or share dreams with a close friend, or join/create a group where the others might act out the different characters. (This needs to be approached with caution as it is important that participants undertake this task with reverence for your images.)

Referring to dream dictionaries is discouraged as they tend to be over-simplistic and cannot by their nature attend to the subtle personal associations and feelings which are key to any understanding of a dream.

You may notice that dreams more usually use images over words to communicate in a concise and precise way with great economy. They are, metaphorically, often like a Japanese painting that communicates an image with minimal strokes of the calligraphic pen. An example of his own that Jung offers is:

> In this dream, a certain Mr X was desperately trying to get behind me and jump on my back. I knew nothing of this gentleman except that he had succeeded in twisting something I had said into a rather grotesque travesty of my meaning.... [t]he dream pointedly brought up the incident again in the apparent 'disguise' of a colloquialism. This saying... "Du kannst mir auf den Buckel steigen" (you can climb on my back)... means "I don't give a damn what you say".
>
> (1961b par. 463)

ANIMALS IN DREAMS

Animals often play a vital role in dreams, acting as powerful symbols. An animal or insect will have quite different connotations for each of us. A different breed might further have more nuanced connotations. If it is your own animal in the dream, this brings it 'closer to home' (see Russack 2002). James Hillman puts it well:

> In many cultures animals do the blessing since they are the divinities. That's why parts of animals are used in medicines and healing rites. Blessing by the animal still goes on in our civilised lives, too. Let's say you have a quick and clever side to your personality. You sometimes lie,

you tend to shoplift, fire excites you, you're hard to track and hard to trap; you have such a sharp nose that people are shy of doing business with you for fear of being outfoxed. Then you dream of a fox! Now that fox isn't merely a "shadow" problem, your propensity to stealth. That fox also gives an archetypal backing to your behavioural traits, placing them more deeply in the nature of things. The fox comes into your dream as a kind of teacher, a doctor animal, who knows lots more than you do about these traits of yours.

(1997 p.2)

American mythologist Joseph Campbell (1904–87) regarded dreams as our own private, personalised, myths and saw myths in contrast as public – depersonalised – dreams (Campbell 1993 p.19). He wrote: "[I]n the dream the forms are quirked by the peculiar troubles of the dreamer; whereas in myth the problems and solutions are directly valid for all mankind" (ibid.). The latter statement requires the caveat that myth is of course culturally specific.

In summary, dreams are a kind of biopsy of the psyche at any given moment (with thanks to the late Dr James Bamber for this evocative expression – personal communication 2008).

EXAMPLE

Let us look at an example of how we might think about a dream from a Jungian perspective and work with it:

I was coming out of an underground tube station and bump into 'A' who was talking about having lost weight. I made a sound of recognition which she acknowledged as me knowing what this was like [indicating a kind of affinity]. *Then there was a remark about someone saying her hair was like a tin hat. It was looking silver grey and like a pudding basin. We were heading in the same direction towards a bridge and then bumped into 'B' and a couple of others joined us as we approached the bridge. It was as if we were on the way to work. It was like going across the wobbly bridge to Tate Modern art gallery from St Paul's Cathedral. But the bridge in the dream was a narrow tarmac strip only really wide enough for one person at a time. As we got on to the bridge we had to take a big step up and we were admiring the trees alongside it, one of which had been trimmed back over the weekend so that the bridge was at the same level as the top of the tree – it was as if we were walking along at the top of the tree* [a reference to my letter to 'C' about being in an elite association]. *A young girl was talking to 'B', looking up to her in admiration. Then a tall man was asking her about holiday places by the sea. 'B' directed him to me for advice about ritzy seaside holidays. I said I needed to hold on to him as we talked as it seemed as if the bridge had changed in that the hand rail had been replaced with a kind of mesh wall leaving nowhere to hold on to. This required balance. The mesh meant that there was no wind buffeting across the bridge. It was rather narrow and felt quite precarious. It was also a bit awkward with the bridge being so narrow but I think we managed to walk and talk as we crossed over the bridge.*

Context and associations:

- Dream is grappling with a worry about a real situation in which the dreamer had written to someone that she is in an elite association, the source of some envy.
- The 'step up' metaphorically refers to a change in life situation.
- Tin hat like a soldier would wear in battle, such as the worrying situation.
- Bridge between attitudes – from 'established' thinking to something more creative?
- Precarious narrow path. Nowhere to hold on to. Difficult, finely balanced task to deal with.
- Only wide enough for one person at a time perhaps refers to Jung's formulation of individuation (see Chapter 4), a path which can only be walked alone, albeit perhaps in the company of other like-minded people, maybe the people who joined the dreamer in crossing the bridge.
- The wobbly nature of the bridge perhaps points to the vulnerable feelings being experienced by the dreamer. In actuality the bridge was repaired so that it was no longer wobbly, perhaps indicating to the dreamer that these feelings too can be 'repaired', ie stabilised and coped with.

Although in Jung's approach to dreams it is useful to think about all the characters as representing different aspects of oneself (and this is where the dialoguing with each character comes in), there is always a so-called dream ego who is the protagonist. It is the person describing the dream as 'I'. Jung's method is to 'circumambulate' the image, looking at the core of the dream image from every angle. For instance, you could try telling the dream (and this could be to yourself possibly by writing the text down) using 'I' but taking each character's perspective in turn, seeing how it looks from this alternative vantage point. You might be surprised how different a situation looks from another position.

So in this example, in broad strokes:

- 'I' is the dream ego, or protagonist.
- 'A' might be seen as the Persona, concern being expressed about her appearance.
- 'B' might be seen as a helpful mother figure.
- 'C' might be seen as a wicked witch character.
- The bridge might be seen as the person's path of individuation itself.

Jung was, with his approach to dreams as in a number of other areas, way ahead of his time. He saw dream analysis as "less a technique than a dialectical process between two personalities" (1961b par.492), which epitomises the Relational approach which has become central in contemporary psychoanalysis.

John Beebe, Jungian analyst based in San Francisco, has developed some interesting ideas for exploring dreams based on his own extension of Jung's theory of Personality Types so that he sees each character in the dream as representing the different psychological characteristics of the dreamer (see Chapter 5).

SUMMARY

- We have looked at the structure and various types of dreams which tend to arise.
- We have seen how Jung built on Freud's original ideas for dream interpretation and went further to formulate his own ideas. These included seeing dreams as compensating for the conscious attitude, which can be worked on using *Active Imagination* and dialoguing with the dream images and symbols.
- Examples have been given of famous instances where dreams were the source of inspiration in writing music and discovering scientific formulae.
- Symbols have been distinguished from signs and semiotics.
- We have explored an example of a dream from a Jungian perspective.
- We have touched on John Beebe's eight-function model as a way of exploring dreams.

The reader is encouraged to keep a workbook, or journal, of your own dreams to see if themes emerge and to help you think about what they might mean, and what value they might have, for you.

REFERENCES

Beebe, J. (2004) "Understanding Consciousness through the Theory of Psychological Types" in *Analytical Psychology: Contemporary Perspectives in Jungian Analysis* (Ed. J. Cambray & L. Carter). Hove: Brunner-Routledge, pp.83–115.

Campbell, J. (1993) *The Hero with a Thousand Faces*. London: Fontana Press.

Freud, S. (1953) "The Interpretation of Dreams" in SE Vol.4.

Freud, S. (1963) "Symbolism in Dreams" in *The Standard Edition of the Complete Psychological Works of Sigmund Freud* (Trans. J. Strachey) (hereafter SE) Vol. 15. London: Hogarth Press, pp.149–169.

George, A. (Trans.) (2000) *The Epic of Gilgamesh*. London: Penguin Classics.

Hillman, J. (1997) *Dream Animals*. San Francisco: Chronicle Books.

Jaffé, A. (1963) *Memories, Dreams, Reflections*. London: Fontana Books.

Jung, C.G. (1913–30) (Ed. S. Shamdasani; Trans. M. Kyburz, J. Peck & S. Shamdasani). *The Red Book: Liber Novus*. London: W.W. Norton, 2009.

Jung, C.G. (1916) "Letter to Fanny Bowditch dated 22nd October 1916" in *C. G. Jung Letters. Vol. 1: 1906–1950* (Ed. G. Adler & A. Jaffé; Trans. R.F.C. Hull). London: Routledge & Kegan Paul, 1973.

Jung, C.G. (1931) "On the Relation of Analytical Psychology to Poetry" in CW15.

Jung, C.G. (1938) "On the Method of Dream Interpretation" in *Children's Dreams: Notes from the Seminar Given in 1936–40*. Princeton, NJ & Oxford: Princeton University Press, 2008.

Jung, C.G. (1946) "Psychology of the Transference" in CW16.

Jung, C.G. (1948a) "On the Nature of Dreams" in CW8.

Jung, C.G. (1948b) "General Aspects of Dream Psychology" in CW8.

Jung, C.G. (1961a) "The Significance of Dreams" in CW18.

Jung, C.G. (1961b) "The Language of Dreams" in CW18.

Jung, C.G. (1973) "Letter to Fanny Bowditch dated 22nd October 1916" in *C. G. Jung Letters Vol. 1, 1906–1950* (Ed. G. Adler & A. Jaffé; Trans. R.F.C. Hull). London: Routledge & Kegan Paul.

Meier, C.A. (1989) *Healing Dream and Ritual*. Einsiedeln: Daimon Verlag, 2003 (3rd edition).

Roberts, R.N. (1989) *Serendipity: Accidental Discoveries in Science*. John Wiley & Sons, Wiley Science Editions.

Russack, N. (2002) *Animal Guides in Life, Myth and Dreams*. Toronto: Inner City Books.

Rycroft, C. (1979) *The Innocence of Dreams*. London: Hogarth Press.

Samuels, A. *et al* (1986) *A Critical Dictionary of Jungian Analysis*. London & New York: Routledge.

Shakespeare, W. (1999) *Hamlet* in *The Oxford Shakespeare: The Complete Works* (Ed. S. Wells & G. Taylor). Oxford: Clarendon Press.

Shamdasani, S. (Ed.) (2009) (Trans. M. Kyburz, J. Peck & S. Shamdasani). *The Red Book: Liber Novus*. London: W.W. Norton & Company.

Stevens, A. (1995) *Private Myths: Dreams and Dreaming*. Cambridge, MA: Harvard University Press, 1997.

Williams, R. (Ed.) (2015) "Jungian Analysis and Humanistic Psychotherapy: Critical Connections Past, Present and Future" in *Self & Society* Vol. 43 No. 3. pp. 197–247.

ALCHEMY AND PSYCHOTHERAPY

"As above, so below."

(Hermes Trismegistus)

WHY ALCHEMY?

You might be wondering what a chapter on alchemy is doing in a book on psychotherapy/psychoanalysis. Jung used alchemy as a metaphor to illuminate his ideas and it proved to be an effective tool. He accumulated a vast library of alchemical tomes which were of profound importance to him:

> The experiences of the alchemists were, in a sense, my experiences
> and their world was my world. This was... a momentous discovery.
> I had stumbled upon the historical counterpart of my psychology of the
> unconscious.

(Jaffé 1963 p.231)

Out of the 20 volumes of Jung's Collected Works, three are dedicated to the study of alchemy. It was clearly of enormous importance to him and formed the major part of his mature work. Jung's work on alchemy describes a process of transformation, or an 'anatomy of individuation' in the words of leading American Jungian analyst Edward Edinger (1922–98), who suggested:

> What makes alchemy so valuable for psychotherapy is that its images
> concretize the experiences of transformation... Alchemy provides a kind
> of anatomy of individuation.
>
> (1994 p.2)

Dale Mathers, a contemporary Jungian analyst and former psychiatrist in London, describes alchemy as "a poetry of science" (2014 p.1), which I hope will begin to give you a sense of the lightness of touch needed to imagine the processes being discussed in this chapter. I do not mean that it is 'make believe' (although it is), but rather that it requires imagination to use metaphor and symbol. The alchemists' search for gold, or the philosopher's stone, can be seen in a psychological sense as finding new insights or symbols and using them in creative and healing ways.

You will find that much of the language of alchemy is rather arcane. Jung switches to using Latin and Ancient Greek with alacrity in his writings as he was fluent in both. Today many of us are unschooled in these languages. I will though keep the Latin and Greek terminology to help you become familiar with Jung's terminology and its use, while providing an English translation into a contemporary idiom.

WHAT IS ALCHEMY?

The alchemists created a *temenos*, or sacred space, out of their laboratory where they carried out ritualised experiments to seek the secret of turning lead into gold, or the philosopher's stone as it was sometimes called in this context. In the literal, historical process of alchemy, fire was applied to a *vas* – or pot – to cook chemical substances and to transform them. The substances would be pulverised with spring dew, which would be mixed with a secret fire – or salt. The mixture would then be placed in a hermetically sealed container – or philosophic egg – and be placed in a furnace. Think of how onion and garlic transform when put into a cooking pot with salt. Their nature changes from a hard, bitter almost inedible vegetable, to a soft, sweet transparent food, which is delicious (if cooked long and slowly enough). The addition of salt draws the water out and aids the cooking process.

The alchemical process is described as follows:

> The [furnace] is devised in such a way as to be able to keep the Egg
> at a constant temperature for long periods of time. The outward fire
> stimulates the action of the inner fire, and must therefore be restrained;
> otherwise, even if the vessel does not break, the whole work will be
> lost. In the initial stage the heat is compared to that of a hen sitting on
> her eggs.
>
> (Klossowski de Rola 1973 p.11)

You might begin to be able to see how these ideas were and are used as a metaphor for the process of working together in analysis. In analysis too we are often sitting patiently while the process 'cooks', which is the precursor to any kind of transformation from one state into another. The cooking may begin outside of the session and 'come to a boil' once the parties meet, which can act as a catalyst for change. This metaphor could of course be applied to any pairing.

ALCHEMICAL STAGES

The alchemist often worked with an assistant – the adept and his *soror mystica*, or spiritual sister (since usually the alchemist was male with a female assistant, though not always). This is important as it brings together the masculine and feminine (see below for discussion of Jung's use of the *Rosarium*).

The process is non-linear and it can begin at any point and go around the cycle of stages any number of times before the satisfaction of completion is achieved. Like *gestalten* (gestalt being the German word for configuration or pattern used by the German-born psychiatrist and psychotherapist Fritz Perls [1893–1970], who developed a method known as Gestalt Therapy), these cycles may apply to particular situations, or the arc of a whole lifetime.

The work of the alchemists was synchronised with the astrological outlook not only to give it the most auspicious chance of success, but in line with the maxim quoted at the beginning of this chapter – "As above, so below". If things are in harmony above (that is, in the heavens), then they will be below on earth. The alchemists recited prayers, and waited for the time to be right to proceed.

The *prima materia* is the raw material of the work, or psychologically – metaphorically – that would refer to the basic matter, or the 'nub of the matter', the problem to be resolved. It is sometimes referred to as the 'black earth'; sometimes the dragon, something to be handled with care but which also guards us.

The work of alchemy is divided into four phases:

FIRST PHASE

The first phase of the work is known as the *nigredo* or blackness. It is also known as the *separatio*, which may be seen as the differentiation of the issues. This phase is ruled by fire. The *nigredo* may be a period of depression (as in Winston Churchill's 'black dog'). It may represent the loneliness often associated with the descent into the path of Individuation (see Chapter 4) in such a deep process of transformation. This period was also seen as a *massa confusa*, referring to the need to disentangle things, a period when you might feel deeply bewildered, as if the ground has gone from under your feet.

Associated with this phase are:

Putrefactio – decay
Calcinatio – incineration, burning
Mortificatio – dying or something dying off

In Jungian terms this phase involves confrontation with the Shadow (see Chapter 3). It culminates when the balance of inner and outer heat mean the *prima materia* is 'cooked', which the alchemists saw as creating a rainbow of beautiful colours corresponding to the stage called the *cauda pavonis* or peacock's tail.

SECOND PHASE

This is known as the *Albedo* – the whitening, the *solutio*, or the *purificatio* – the purification. This phase is ruled by water. Tears may be shed. It concerns regeneration (like watering a plant), awakening, opening the heart, cleansing the soul. Feelings need to be accepted. Its symbol is the moon, shining in the darkness as consciousness awakens.

Baring:

> In vivid imagery [the alchemists] describe the process of transforming the *prima materia* of the initial psychic state by repeated washings,

> cleansings, purifications, repeated immersions in water and repeated
> submissions to the heating power of fire which together separate out
> and remove the rust... which had accrued to and hidden the gold of the
> spirit.
>
> (2013 p.481)

A spark of light – insight – may appear on the horizon. This is the
beginning of synthesis.

THIRD PHASE

This phase is known as the *citronitas* or yellowing. There are transpersonal tasks to be undertaken. In some models this phase is excluded
or seen as a part of the next phase.

FOURTH PHASE

This final phase is known as the *rubedo* or reddening; or the *coniunctio*,
meaning reunification. This relates to the reunion of body, soul and
spirit. Inner conflict lessens. The reddening evokes the sky at sunrise
and the dawn of new possibilities. Red is the colour of the *rubedo* and
symbolises the completion of the cycle, represented by the phoenix
rising from the ashes of our old ways.

These phases have to be repeated as many times as need be, as in
analysis. I will end this section with a salutary reminder from Ann
Baring:

> We grow through the *Nigredo* and *Albedo* phases of alchemy into the
> *Rubedo*. We cannot force entry into it by spiritual exercises or any
> formulation of goals. It may happen to us... or we can grow into it
> through the expansion of the heart, the instinctive capacity to love, to
> give to others, to serve life through an awakened compassion.
>
> (2013 pp.482–3)

IN PSYCHOLOGICAL TERMS

Alchemy is about reviving or re-finding spirit in matter. In entering
into the work of alchemy we join with spirit to release its energy.
And in healing ourselves, we heal the world as we are connected. We
are all a part of the *unus mundus* (one world). We all stem from the

same source. So exploring oneself in therapy can become more than a private matter. It can have ramifications for our families, communities and society as a whole.

The search for the philosopher's stone – the gold of insight – symbolises the stages in the journey of analysis, through the struggles to heal and to reunite – body, soul and spirit – within the Self. Ann Baring expresses this from the depth of her immersion in this material for over 50 years in her uniquely poetic way:

> Alchemy flows beneath the surface of Western civilization like a river of gold, preserving its images and its insights for us... Alchemy builds a rainbow bridge between the human and the divine, the seen and unseen dimensions of reality, between matter and spirit
>
> (2013 p.457)

She sees alchemy as a spiritual process whereby the cosmos itself:

> calls to us to become aware that we participate in its life... everything is sacred and connected: one life; one spirit... tasks us... to awaken the divine spark of our consciousness and reunite it in the invisible Soul of the Cosmos.
>
> (2013 pp.457–8)

She goes further. Baring sees alchemy as changing our very perception of reality and addressing the questions everyone has at some point in their life:

> "who are we?" and "why are we here?" It refines and transmutes the base metal of our understanding so that we – evolved from the very substance of the stars – can know that we participate in the mysterious ground of spirit while living in this physical dimension of reality.
>
> (2013 p.458)

The analyst's consulting room – as the alchemists' laboratory – has to be prepared with care. The frame of the analytic *temenos* needs attention to ensure it is private, clean (both physically and of intrusive negative energies) and is a safe and comfortable space both for the person consulting the analyst and for the analyst him or herself who needs to pay heed to ensure they have sufficient free attention to attend to the person coming to see them: phones need to be turned off, intrusive noises minimised, the analyst's own troubles put aside.

CASE EXAMPLES

To bring this down to earth, it may help to look at the case of a woman I will refer to as Sophie to see how these processes work in practical reality and how useful alchemy can prove as a clinical tool. Sophie had been in analysis for many years working at depth. The image of the spiral is helpful in understanding the ever-deepening layers of these processes. It could seem as if you are going around in circles looking at the same old issues, whereas, thinking about the work of analysis as a spiral, you are looking at sometimes known issues but from different perspectives. This is why analysis can last a long time. There are always more facets, more depths to explore. Sophie thought about this as an image of a Russian doll: "Each time I get hurt, a doll breaks and I get further down to the core". Sophie found herself suddenly – literally overnight – engulfed in a traumatic family situation. At least, it seemed to appear overnight; in fact the problem had been bubbling under the surface over many years. But it was like an explosion in a chemical factory; a lightening bolt severing her connection to the family. The fire of *calcinatio* erupted and catalysed a brutal inferno. She grieved and raged for 18 months, periodically reaching new insights and having breakthroughs in understanding. (One phase of *nigredo*.) We thought about the family alchemically as an interconnected system (an *unus* mundus) where, if one part is damaged, the whole is damaged; if one part suffers loss, so does the whole. The rest of the family scapegoated her and attributed all this negativity to her alone but their linear thinking did not make sense. Spiritual – interrelated – connection was missing. She realised the feelings being experienced on all sides related to a family trauma going back to the Holocaust (the light of this understanding creating a door to the *Albedo*). When she put this idea to the family, it was reviled and could not be acknowledged. Tragically, a niece's marriage broke down. It became clear that the trauma was spreading. The symptoms of the syndrome relating to being Holocaust survivors were becoming apparent in the grandchildren of the original Holocaust survivor, which made it more possible for the whole family unit to experience the trauma and realise that there was some truth in what she was saying (*rubedo*). This brought about a significant shift and began to usher in some peace.

The following quote describes the process Sophie was thrown into, which almost literally led her to death's door before things could turn around:

> The alchemist descended into the depths of his soul to undergo a death and rebirth, to transform his consciousness from base metal into gold... it was the images and dreams that came to him as he did this work which reflected what was taking place in the vessel of his own soul and alerted him to, then deepened his understanding of the process of psychic transformation.
>
> (Baring 2013 p.468)

As so often – and it is difficult to remember this in the midst of a crisis – dawning awareness of the family trauma was the threshold to a new orientation, an enhanced quality of life invigorated by a new relationship to spirit and soul with which Sophie had been forced to engage. Using the alchemical metaphor as a framework to understand these matters seemed helpful and put private troubles into a wider, perhaps universal, context. Sometimes it is the stages set out above that prove helpful in thinking about a case; sometimes the colours associated with each stage become significant for instance as they arise in dreams. Alchemy provides a complex and rich palette of images and ideas on which to draw.

A second example: Rachel's first Jungian analyst was a man to whom she felt a strong erotic charge. She dreamt: *[the analyst] was in the bath and beckoning me to join him.* This felt exciting and meaningful to her. You will see below in the section on Jung's engagement with the *Rosarium Philosphorum* how the image of being in the bath can represent being involved in the process of alchemical transformation, being steeped in a process/substance.

HISTORICAL ROOTS

I will now lay out a brief history of alchemy. Alchemy pre-dates science, and is the forerunner of chemistry, at least 4,000 years old. Texts have been discovered from Egyptian, Babylonian, Greek, Arab and Persian sources.

Ann Baring sets out the names of the great alchemists who have formed a chain dating back to the eighth century passing on the secrets of this ancient art/science. I will list them here to honour their contributions and to familiarise you with their names:

> Geber or Jabir – eighth-century alchemist who lived at the Court of Harun al-Rashid in Baghdad; founder of Chemistry who had an immense influence on European alchemists.
>
> Rhazes, Rasis or Al-Razi (c. 825–c. 924), Persia
>
> Roger Bacon (1220–92), England
>
> Albertus Magnus (1200–80), Germany
>
> Arnold of Villanova (1235–1311), Spain
>
> Raymond Lull (1232–1316), Deia, Majorca
>
> Nicholas Flamel (1330–1413), Paris
>
> Basil Valentine – German, 17th century (this name may be an alias)
>
> Salomon Trismosin, 16th century, author of an exquisite manuscript, the *Splendor Soli* – one of the treasures of the British Library.
>
> Paracelsus (1493–1541), Swiss
>
> Gerhard Dorn (1530–84), Belgian
>
> Giordano Bruno (1548–1600), Italian (burnt at the stake in 1600)
>
> (Baring 2013 pp.462–3)

Alchemists saw themselves as servants to the work; humility was and remains a key attitude. Patience is essential. This is seen in stark contrast to the modern haste epitomised in the manualised and short-term psychotherapy services currently being promoted for their scientific 'evidence base'. Even the terminology speaks to its severed connection to soul.

The alchemists in their laboratories were not necessarily or always looking for literal gold. They used these methods or ideas symbolically. Manuscripts recently discovered by Zosimus of Panopolis dating back to AD third century show that even then, alchemy was regarded as the art of soul transmutation, rather than literal transformation of base metals into gold (Baring 2013 pp. 461–2). Indeed, those who approached alchemy through greed and intellect alone were known as puffers (Bygott 2014 p. 30). Bygott explains:

> we have to be willing to hover between manifest life and its subtle essence through metaphor and symbol. Indian Vedic philosophy describes it as the eternal dance between Shiva (essence) and Shakti (form). Chinese Taoist philosophy pictures it as the Yang/Yin symbol which provides the fundamental structure of the 'I Ching (Book of Changes)' (Wilhelm 1951). Alchemists describe it as the *Mysterium*

Coniunctionis, the sacred marriage of *Sol* and *Luna*, the solar and lunar principles. Jung's analytic psychology describes it as the masculine/feminine *Dance of Opposites*.

(ibid.)

We will now meet *Sol* and *Luna* in Jung's work on the *Rosarium*.

JUNG AND THE *ROSARIUM*

The *Rosarium Philosophorum* (or rose garden of the philosophers) is an alchemical text dating back to 1550 which contains a series of woodcut images. Jung writes a commentary on ten of them in volume 16 of his Collected Works to illustrate his thinking about the phenomenon of transference. He uses the set of images as a metaphor to describe the process of transference in analysis. The series of images contain representations of the 'mystical marriage' (the *heirosgamos*) of masculine and feminine (although this does not mean necessarily that the relationship to which they are applied need be literally between a man and a woman).

MERCURIAL FOUNTAIN

The series begins with the image of the mercurial fountain. The element Mercury is also known as quicksilver and is associated with the Greek god Hermes, invoked when the substances are hermetically sealed in the alchemical *vas* (container). Jung saw mercury – with its paradoxical qualities – as representing the unconscious. Hermes is quick and mercurial in nature, swift-footed with winged feet, changing [things] quixotically.

Jung describes this woodcut (Figure 7.1) as a quadratic quarternity (a 'four of fours'), with four stars in the corners representing the four elements. The base of the fountain represents the alchemists' *vas*, the container where the substances intermingle and transform. It contains the 'divine water' representing chaos in this instance. You will notice the 'frame' of the image is square, the vessel circular, bringing together two shapes which always form part of a mandala (see Chapter 4). Alchemists saw the circle as the

ROSARIVM

Wyr sindt der metall anfang vnd erste natur /
Die kunst macht durch vns die höchste tinctur.
Keyn brunn noch wasser ist meyn gleych /
Ich mach gesund arm vnd reych.
Vnd bin doch jtzund gyfftig vnd dötlich.

Succus

Figure 7.1   The mercurial fountain

perfect form as opposed to the square, which needs to transform in this image (as in the colloquial expressions that someone needs the rough edges knocked off, or that you cannot fit a square peg into a round hole).

The inscription around the fountain's rim reads: 'Unus est Mercurious mineralis, Mercurious vegatalis, Mercurious animalis', meaning the world is divided into mineral, vegetable and animal; the three parts of the philosophy of the whole world are contained in the single stone, namely the Mercurious of the philosophers (1946 par. 402). These same words – animal, vegetable and mineral – also appear around the top of the frame.

On the outside of the vessel there are six stars. Together with Mercurious these represent the seven planets or metals. All the world is here. The three outlets of the fountain represent the three manifestations of mercury, and his triune nature. Mercury is sometimes shown as a three-headed serpent. Above the fountain are the sun and the moon. They often appear in these images as symbols of male (sun) and female (moon), representing gold and silver, respectively. Between them lies a further star, which Jung interprets as representing the 'quintessential star', a symbol of the unity of the four hostile elements (Jung 1946 par. 403).

At the top of the frame is a two-headed serpent representing the devil. This is suggested by Gerhard Dorn (1530–84), the alchemist to whom Jung most often refers. (Dorn was a pupil of Paracelsus who published various alchemical texts between 1565 and 1578). The heads are spitting fire, which initiates the alchemical process. The fire also burns up the bad odours and vapours in the laboratory, cleansing the environment in preparation for the work, just as you might clean up before visitors are expected.

> This structure reveals the... (fourfold nature) of the transforming process... It begins with the four separate elements, the state of chaos, and ascends by degrees to the three manifestations of Mercurious in the inorganic, organic and spiritual worlds; and after attaining the form of Sol and Luna (i.e. the precious metals gold and silver...) it culminates in the one and indivisible... nature of the *anima*[soul]... or *lapis philosophorum* [philosopher's stone].

> (Jung 1946 par. 404)

Notice that this illustrates a progression from 4 to 3 to 2 to 1. This motif appears throughout alchemy and was a pattern which became important to Jung for its spiritual acuity. It is called the axiom of Maria after Maria Prophetissa (sometimes known as the Jewess, sister of Moses, or the Copt), who lived in third-century Alexandria (then the intellectual capital of the Roman Empire) and is a significant figure in alchemy.

The woodcut sets us out on our path with a symbolic picture of the methods and philosophy of alchemy.

KING AND QUEEN

The next woodcut is the king and queen standing on the sun and moon, respectively. Jung suggests the initial meeting is distant as they are wearing formal courtly clothes. They give each other their left hand rather than their right because a left handshake indicates a secret. And the secret here is the king and queen are brother and sister so that this is incest. (Using the images as a metaphor for connection helps to remove any element concerning the morality of this relationship.) In their right hands they each hold a branch with two flowers. These together symbolise the four elements: fire and air (which are active); water and earth (which are passive). The first two are ascribed to the male; the second to the female. The fifth flower comes from above delivered by a dove Jung sees as analogous to Noah's dove, which carried the olive branch of reconciliation (ibid. par. 410) or the union of this pair. The dove descends from the quintessential star (like the one between sun and moon in the image of the mercurial fountain). The three branches allude to the three spouts in the mercurial fountain in the previous image.

In the original Latin text beneath the royal couple says:

> Mark well, in the art of our magisterium nothing is concealed by the philosophers except the secret of the art which may not be revealed to all and sundry. For were that to happen, that man would be accursed; he would incur the wrath of God and perish of apoplexy. Wherefore all error in the art arises because men do not begin with the proper substance, and for this reason you should employ the venerable Nature, because from her and through her and in her is our art born and in naught else; and so our magisterium is the work of Nature and not of the worker.

(ibid. par. 411)

PHILOSOPHORVM.

Nota bene: In arte noſtri magiſterij nihil eſt ſecretum celatū à Philoſophis excepto ſecreto artis, quod artis non licet cuiquam reuelare, quod ſi fieret ille ma ledicerctur , & indignationem domini incur= reret, & apoplexia moreretur. Quare om= nis error in arte exiſtit , ex eo, quod debitam

C ij

Figure 7.2 The king and queen

Jung says that the flowers represent projections on to each other of *anima* and *animus* (see Chapter 3) as soul partners. Their intermingling souls form a spiritual marriage. Psychologically speaking, this is equivalent to – yet not identical with – a transferential relationship in analysis.

THE NAKED TRUTH

The (abridged) text in the original which runs across the top of the third woodcut reads (with Jung's own alterations to the quote):

> He who would be initiated into this art and secret wisdom must put away the vice of arrogance, must be devout, righteous, deep-witted, humane towards his fellows, of a cheerful countenance and a happy disposition, and respectful withal.

(ibid. par. 450)

This is the attitude required to do the work.

Jung continues: "The chaste disguises have fallen away. Man and woman confront one another in unabashed naturalness" (ibid. par. 451). The dove is again above and between the couple carrying a branch. The left hands are no longer touching. Now Luna's left hand and Sol's right hand hold the branches as their opposite hands touch the flowers, the uniting symbol. There are now three flowers, not five. Jung sees the throwing off of their outer vestments as signifying throwing off conventions. No adornments are necessary. People are seen as they really are. Animal instincts become more conscious.

IMMERSION IN THE BATH

The fourth woodcut shows the couple together in the alchemical bath (drawn as a hexagonal structure which looks like a Jacuzzi). This takes us back to the mercurial fountain: "The rising fountain of the unconscious has reached the king and queen, or rather they have descended into it as into a bath" (ibid. par. 453). Jung sees the immersion in water as relating to the alchemical '*solutio*', perhaps also the solution of a problem. He likens the water to the amniotic fluid in a womb, for the alchemists sometimes referred to the *vas* as a uterus and its content as a foetus (ibid. par. 454).

PHILOSOPHORVM.

seipsis secundum æqualitatē inspissentur. Solus enim calor tēperatus est humiditatis inspissatiuus et mixtionis perfectiuus, et non super excedens. Nã generatiões et procreationes rerū naturaliũ habent solũ fieri per tēperatissimũ calorē et æqua lē, vti est solus fumus equinus humidus et calidus.

Figure 7.3 The naked truth

ROSARIVM

corrũpitur, neǆ ex imperfecto penitus secundũ artem aliquid fieri poteſt. Ratio eſt quia ars prĩ mas diſpoſitiones inducere non poteſt, ſed lapis noſter eſt res media inter perfecta & imperfecta corpora, & quod natura ipſa incepit hoc per artem ad perfectionẽ deducitur. Si in ipſo Mercurio operari inceperis vbi natura reliquit imperfectum, inuenies in eo perfectionẽ et gaudebis.

Perfectum non alteratur, ſed corrumpitur. Sed imperfectum bene alteratur, ergo corruptio vnius eſt generatio alterius.

Speculum

Figure 7.4   Immersion in the bath

The couple are still holding on to their branches, the king with his left hand and the queen now with her right. They each touch the other's flower with their opposite hands. Once again the dove above sits between them and his branch still crosses theirs pointing downwards.

The queen stands for body; the king for spirit. Soul embodies the love between them. The dove from above and the water from below link to the soul:

> The unrelated human being lacks wholeness, for he can achieve wholeness only through the soul, and the soul cannot exist without its other side, which is always found in a "You".

(ibid.)

Psychologically, the picture is seen as a descent, an immersion into the unconscious.

THE CONJUNCTION

The fifth woodcut depicts the union between the couple.

They are naked, entwined in each other's arms. The two are made as one, floating in water which Jung links here to the unconscious. King and queen, *Sol* and *Luna*, are now winged – they have become spirit. With alchemy we are constantly dealing with paradox. Water is linked to fire and thence to steam, relating this to the boiling solution in which the two substances symbolised by *Sol* and *Luna* unite in the alchemical *vas*. Union is seen as the time when marvels occur, when the philosopher's stone is begotten. The *contiunctio*, the joining of the couple, "brings to birth something that is one and united" (ibid. par. 458).

DEATH

In the sixth woodcut the king and queen lie dead in an oblong bath. The changed shape of the bath alludes to the transformation. The vas, the fountain and the sea have become their tomb.

They have become a single being with two heads. The right side of the body is male and the left female. One crown encircles both their

CONIVNCTIO SIVE
Coitus.

O Luna durch meyn vmbgeben/vnd suſſe mynne/
Wirſtu ſchön/ ſtarck/ vnd gewaltig als ich byn.

O Sol/ du biſt vber alle liecht zu erkennen/
So bedarffſtu doch mein als der han der hennen.

ARISLEVS IN VISIONE.

Coniunge ergo filium tuum Gabricum dile=
ctiorem tibi in omnibus filijs tuis cum ſua ſorore
Beya

Figure 7.5 The conjunction

PHILOSOPHORVM.

CONCEPTIO SEV PVTRE
factio

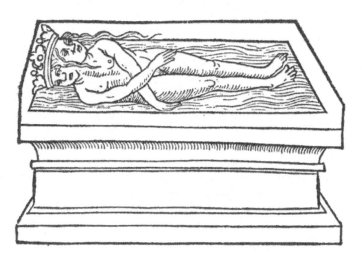

Hye ligen könig vnd köningin dot/
Die sele scheydt sich mit grosser not.

ARISTOTELES REX ET
Philosophus.

Nunquam vidi aliquod animatum crescere
sine putrefactione, nisi autem fiat putri=
dum inuanum erit opus alchimicum.

Figure 7.6 Death

heads. This woodcut represents the *putrefactio*, the decay of the body. Paradoxically the image is headed 'conception', a reference to the cycle of life, death leading to rebirth. New life cannot arise without the death of the old. A new attitude cannot be accommodated until old ideas are put aside. A new relationship cannot be fully begun before the unfinished business of old alliances are dealt with.

THE ASCENT OF THE SOUL

Putrefactio continues until the soul mounts to heaven, depicted in the seventh woodcut. There is only one soul as the two are now united. In the woodcut the pair are joined as one, still in the oblong tomb, with an image of the soul rising into heaven.

PURIFICATION

The eighth woodcut depicts the royal pair in their oblong tomb, still joined as one. Dew falls from the sky, which Jung sees as a portent of the divine birth which is to come. The water helps to cleanse and purify.

THE RETURN OF THE SOUL

In the ninth woodcut the royal pair in their tomb are united as one. The soul is shown diving back down towards the couple to breathe life back into their body.

Two birds are shown at the bottom of the woodcut; one standing on the ground, the other partly buried with only its head above the surface. Jung links these to the allegorical winged and wingless dragons, a reference back to the double nature of Mercurious (remember the double-headed dragon in the first woodcut of the mercurial fountain spitting fire). The two birds are separate entities in the image in contrast to the hermaphroditic figure of the couple, signifying the problem of uniting the opposites is not yet over.

Jung:

> In alchemy the purification is the result of numerous distillations; in psychology too it comes from an equally thorough separation of the ordinary ego-personality from all inflationary admixtures of unconscious

ROSARIVM
ANIMÆ EXTRACTIO VEL
imprægnatio

Hye teylen sich die vier element/
Aus dem leyb scheydt sich die sele behendt.

De

Figure 7.7 Ascent of the soul

PHILOSOPHORVM

ABLVTIO VEL
Mundificatio

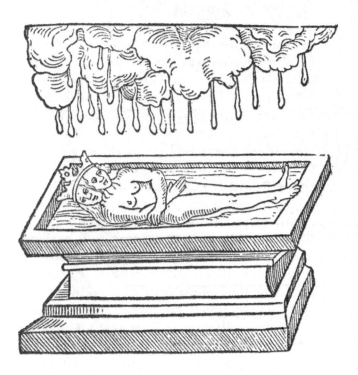

Hie felt der Tauw von himmel herab/
Vnnd wafcht den fchwarßen leyb im grab ab.

K . iij

Figure 7.8 Purification

PHILOSOPHORVM

ANIMÆ IVBILATIO SEV
Ortus seu Sublimatio.

hie schwingt sich die sele hernidder/
Vnd erquickt den gereinigten leychnam wider.

L iij

Figure 7.9   Return of the soul

PHILOSOPHORVM.

Hie ist geboren die eddele Keyserin reich/
Die meister nennen sie jhrer dochter gleich.
Die vermeret sich/gebiert kinder ohn zal/
Sein vndötlich rein/vnnd ohn alles mahl.

Dis

Figure 7.10 The New Birth

material. This task entails the most painstaking self-examination and self-education... The process of psychological differentiation is no light work; it needs the tenacity and patience of the alchemist.

(1946 par. 503)

THE NEW BIRTH

The final woodcut in the series, the tenth, depicts the royal couple arisen out of the tomb. The work is complete. The figure is known as the rebis representing the unity of the Self. They now stand upright and are out of the bath.

The figure has become an androgyne (as in androgenous) (rather than a hermaphrodite), which unites male and female in a conscious way, being both separate and together. The difference is subtle: in a hermaphrodite, male and female are unconsciously joined and the hermaphrodite can only unite with itself. The androgyne in contrast unites the two consciously; they are both separate and together (Mathers 2014 p.55).

The figure stands on the moon. The right-hand side of the figure is male; the left female. Its wings indicate its spiritual nature, an ability to soar. In one hand it holds a chalice containing three snakes representing *Mercurious* (or possibly one snake with three heads). In the other hand is a single snake. This brings us back to the image of four, which Jung sees as so significant in representing wholeness. Jung regards snakes in this image as pointing to the problem of evil. To the left of the figure we find a raven, denoting the devil. The half-buried, unfledged bird, from the previous woodcut has disappeared.

To the right of the figure is a 'sun and moon tree', which Jung interprets as representing the conscious equivalent of the unconscious processes of development suggested on the other side of the figure.

The woodcuts can all be viewed online using a search for 'rosarium philosophorum images' where they appear in colour.

WHAT DOES ALCHEMY ADD TO OUR UNDERSTANDING?

In drawing this chapter to a close, it is important to ask what does alchemy add that would otherwise be absent? It is a framework like many others which helps us understand psychological processes and does so in its own unique way. The images are not 'factual' but symbolic and evocative, invoking ideas, fantasy, musing, wondering. It invokes the imagination to see things in a poetical way, which strikes a chord with the unconscious so we can experience its truths.

Alchemy does not force. It describes what '*is*' in a way which makes felt sense, even though we have to find our way through such unwieldy language. (The nature of the language itself is deliberate in that it reflects the nature of the unconscious.) The style communicates something important. We know by the florid language that we are in a world of imagination, something akin to a fairy tale or myth. We know we are not speaking 'ordinary' language, although we can apply these ideas to the mundane world in which we live.

SUMMARY

We have looked at how alchemy can provide such suitable metaphors for psychological work and the transference relationship in particular. We have gone through the various stages required to transform the psyche. Historical roots give a sense of the ancient nature of this art/science, which has been contrasted with similar practices in other cultures. Clinical examples from contemporary practice show how these ideas may appear and be applied in the present day. Alchemy offers an 'anatomy of the psyche'. We then looked in detail at Jung's use of the *Rosarium Philosophorum* and his deep engagement with the images of transformation set out in the ancient woodcut images.

REFERENCES

Baring, A. (2013) *The Dream of the Cosmos: A Quest for the Soul.* Dorset: Archive Publishing.

Bygott, C. (2014) "Mysterium Coniunctionis" in *Alchemy and Psychotherapy: Post-Jungian Perspectives* (Ed. D. Mathers). London & New York: Routledge. pp. 27–43.

Edinger, E. (1994) *Anatomy of the Psyche: Alchemical Symbolism in Psychotherapy.* Chicago & La Salle, IL: Open Court.

Jaffé, A. (1963) *Memories, Dreams, Reflections*. London: Fontana Press, 1995.

Jung, C.G. (1946) "Psychology of the Transference" in CW 16.

Klossowski de Rola, S. (1973) *Alchemy: The Secret Art*. London: Thames and Hudson.

Mathers, D. (Ed.) (2014) *Alchemy and Psychotherapy: Post-Jungian Perspectives*. London & New York: Routledge.

JUNG: POLITICS, PROBLEMS AND IN THE WORLD

Since Jung's death in 1961, his ideas have been revised to counter certain biases contained in the original work to reflect contemporary thinking. This final chapter covers a range of topics in the Jungian field where there are problems (race, including accusations of anti-Semitism and gender), as well as solutions.

I then refer more briefly to nascent areas of interest (ecopsychology and man's relationship with animals) which have begun to emerge from the field and where Jungian ideas are of use.

Finally, I look at the ways in which Jungian ideas are being applied in the world and in politics, including a growing move towards political activism and thinking more radically about how Jungian psychology may be of use.

So this chapter covers four distinct areas. Inevitably there is insufficient space in one chapter to discuss all these topics in depth. I am therefore pointing to directions for further study if this piques your interest.

(1) JUNG AND RACE/ISM

In 1988 the Jungian community was rocked when Farhad Dalal (non-Jungian psychotherapist in Britain) mounted an eviscerating attack on Jung's psychology of race in his paper entitled "Jung: A Racist" (1988), which has become the most frequently downloaded paper from the *British Journal of Psychotherapy*. There is no doubt that Jung's pronouncements on race were unfortunate. Dalal contends:

[Jung] *explicitly* equates:

1.   The modern black with the prehistoric human
2.   The modern black conscious with the white unconscious
3.   The modern black adult with the white child

(1988 pp.263–79)

Jung had a deep interest in exploring race, culture and religion. He travelled widely to meet people in India, Africa and in Arizona and New Mexico to spend time with Native peoples. While in the United States he had a particular interest in working with African-Americans, and analysed about 15 on his trip. This could be seen as patronising, but it is remarkable in his milieu for him to have had such an interest.

Jung's thinking on race leaves much for contemporary Jungians to revise as some of his ideas are out of register with contemporary mores. Jung's theoretical model is eloquently encapsulated by Samuels when he discusses a shocking diagram – a genealogical tree – created by Jolande Jacobi in *The Psychology of C. G. Jung* published in 1942 with Jung's express approval. Samuels summarises: "Jung asserted that there is a 'collective psyche limited to race, tribe, and family over and above the "universal" collective psyche'" (1993 p.308).

Figure 8.1 shows the diagram:

Jacobi (quoted in Samuels) describes her diagram as follows:

> At the very bottom lies the unfathomable, the central force out of which at one time the individual psyche has been differentiated. This central force goes through all further differentiations and isolations, lives in them all, cuts through them to the individual psyche.
>
> (Samuels 1993 p.308)

Samuels then goes on:

> Resting on this 'unfathomable ground', Jacobi arranges different strata; there are eight in all, arranged like the layers of a cake: the central force, animal ancestors, primitive human ancestors, groups of people, nation, tribe, family, individual
>
> (ibid.)

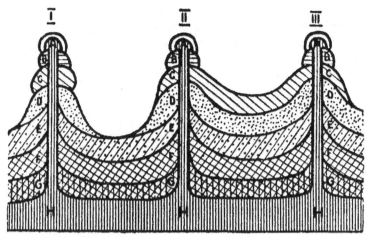

Figure 8.1 Jacobi's 'psychic genealogical tree'
Source: Diagram from Jolande Jacobi, *The Psychology of C.G. Jung* (New Haven, CT: Yale University Press, 1973), diagram XI, p.34. Copyright 1973 by Yale University Press.

This might be seen as relatively innocuous to the casual reader, until it becomes clear there is value and priority attached to the order of the layers and, although Jacobi does not actually mention 'race', it is important to read carefully:

> it is clear from the text as well as from Jung's remarks that this is what is meant by 'groups of people'... referred [to]... in the post-war edition as 'ethnic group'.
>
> (Samuels 1993 p.308)

There has been an attempt in recent years to formulate an apology or a statement from the professional community of Jungians for these unfortunate, discredited views. However, this has met with obstacles which we are trying to surmount.

ANTI-SEMITISM

The story of Jung's purported association with Nazism and his alleged anti-Semitism needs to be both acknowledged and systematically addressed on two fronts: in terms of his (i) thinking/theorising, and (ii) actions. I go into considerable detail here to focus on certain key moments and statements which are the most noteworthy so as to be transparent about Jung's past. These are:

(A) THE NEOPAGAN/VOLKISCH ROOTS OF ANALYTICAL PSYCHOLOGY

The roots of Jung's early psychology were growing in the same soil as National Socialism historically. He came from the same Central European cultures that brought about the Nazi movement.

(B) JUNG'S RADIO BROADCAST

In 1933 Jung gave a radio interview in which he refers to Hitler in terms that it is difficult to see as less than admiring. Matthias von der Tann made a careful linguistic analysis of Jung's remarks, which he believes constitute a message: "Jung supports the Nazi cause" (Samuels 1991 p.197).

(C) ASSUMING PRESIDENCY OF THE GENERAL SOCIETY AND EDITORSHIP OF THE ZENTRALBLATT

Six months after Hitler came to power, Jung was asked to become the president of the General Medical Society for Psychotherapy as Jews were being deposed of positions of power (although in fact his predecessor was not Jewish). He agreed to serve as president on condition the organisation was renamed the International General Medical Society for Psychotherapy and that it was "reconstituted to enable Jewish psychotherapists barred from the German national section to join the international society directly as individual members with equal rights" (Vannoy Adams and Sherry 1991 p.366). There is a divergence of opinion as to whether this was an astute political move on Jung's part to enable his Jewish colleagues to continue with their professional affiliation (Jaffé 1989, Maidenbaum 1991), or whether Jung was gripped by the Shadow and opportunistically fulfilling leadership ambitions (Samuels 1991).

In September 1933 Matthias Heinrich Göring (cousin of Hermann, second in command to Hitler), an Adlerian analyst, became president of a newly constituted German General Medical Society for Psychotherapy. Jung and Göring thus became colleagues. Jung was present at a 1934 congress where Göring made a speech endorsing Hitler's *Mein Kampf* (Samuels 1993). Jung and Göring jointly authored a tribute praising Dr Sommer, whose works can only be described as deeply racist.

Concurrently with these events Jung had become the psychotherapy profession's journal editor. He published a paper which spoke in a more or less admiring manner of the "powerful phenomenon of National Socialism" and in which he further stressed a distinction between German and Jewish psychology. His timing could not have been more ill-judged if he did not want to be linked with Nazi ideology on race. Siegmund Hurwitz (a Kabbalah scholar and Jung's dentist who was in analysis with Jung for 10 years) reportedly "told Jung how troubled he was by some of Jung's earlier writings on the Jewish psyche, including the timing of his 1934 article. Jung's reply to Dr Hurwitz was: 'Today I would not write this article in this way. I have written in my long life many books, and I have also written nonsense. Unfortunately, that was nonsense'" (Maidenbaum 1991 p.295).

(D) ENGEL'S TESTIMONY

Werner Engel (psychiatrist, Jungian analyst, Jewish refugee from the Nazi regime) provides the most affecting of testimonies (Maidenbaum & Martin (1991). His own mother committed suicide (the day before she was due to receive from Engel in the post a visa and ticket to the United States) after she had received an order to report to a concentration camp. He remembers Jung giving a seminar in 1934 Berlin. Jung stood with a Nazi flag on his left and a Nazi officer sitting to his right. (It was customary for such events to be monitored in this manner.) Intuitively such a scene elicits revulsion and one might easily condemn Jung for agreeing to such conditions. Engel goes on to describe, however, Jung expressing an ambiguous sentiment within the earshot of the Nazi officer about a military parade passing by the window in the middle of this seminar at which Mussolini was being received by Hitler. This could easily have compromised Jung's personal safety. The question remains, however – why did Jung proceed with his seminar on this basis?

(E) JUNG'S APOLOGY TO LEO BAECK (1873–1956)

After German Rabbi Leo Baeck was freed from the concentration camp, he met up with Jung again. In the course of an extended conversation during which Rabbi Baeck confronted Jung head on, Jung acknowledged "Well, I slipped up", which Baeck accepted.

(F) PSYCHOLOGY OF RACE

In "The Role of the Unconscious" (1918 p.3–28) Jung distinguishes between Jewish and Germanic (or 'Aryan') psychology. He says "The soil of any country holds some mystery. Just as there is a relationship of mind and body, so there is a relationship of body to earth" (1918 p.13). Following this line of thought he sees Jews as suffering for want of their own land (and goes so far as to imply Jews are like parasites that need a 'host' nation [1934 par. 353]). Jung was a supporter of Zionism for reasons explained in his 1918 paper. He extrapolates from these notions ideas which are capable of being construed negatively.

Jung scholar Geoffrey Cocks tells us an article in the journal *Rasse* in 1939 "equated Jung's notion of the collective unconscious with the Nazi concept of heredity and race. This article was listed on the official Nazi party bibliography" (1991 p.162), thereby demonstrating how Jung's views were at the very least hijacked by the Nazis.

(G) JUNG AS WAR CRIMINAL

In 1946 claims were made by the disgruntled husband of one of Jung's analysands accusing Jung of having connections with the Nazis. There were even proposals to put Jung on trial as a war criminal (Roazen 1991 p.218–19).

Others (such as the historian Roepke) have suggested that Jung was courted by the Nazis. James Kirsch explodes that myth when he reports on a visit to Berlin in May 1933:

> Jung was invited to see Dr Goebbels, the infamous minister of propaganda. Jung went and the following conversation occurred:
>
> Goebbels: You wanted to see me, Dr Jung.
> Jung: No. You wanted to see me.

> Goebbels:No.You wanted to see me.
>
> Jung turned around and left Goebbels' office – and vomited!!!
>
> (1991 p.77)

Kirsch closes the matter by explaining: "This was the end of the 'courting' of Jung by the Nazis" (ibid. p.77). Although of course this could be variously interpreted, Kirsch (himself a refugee from the Nazis) is a reliable source.

Agent 488

Other accounts indicate that, far from being a Nazi collaborator, Jung was enlisted as an agent for the Allies. Jung was dubbed 'Agent 488' by Allen Dulles, an American agent who recruited spies against Nazi Germany (Bair 2003 p.486). He regularly sought Jung's advice. Dulles credited Jung with helping him to understand the situation, saying "He [Jung] [understood] the characteristics of the sinister leaders of Nazi Germany and Fascist Italy.... His deep antipathy to what Nazism and Fascism stood for was clearly evidenced in these conversations" (ibid. p.493).

Jung and Hitler

Deirdre Bair (Jung's biographer) cites reports and rumours about Jung's direct dealings with Hitler and concludes that Jung's involvement "was peripheral" (ibid. p.482). Bair's voluminous evidence boils down to the fact that, in the summer of 1942, one of Hitler's physicians asked Jung to examine Hitler. Jung declined and his excuses were accepted (ibid.).

(H) PERSONAL RELATIONSHIP TO JUDAISM AND FREUD

Jung's relationship to Freud is significant. Before the rift between them, there was a deep bond and mutual recognition.

There is no doubt that Jung clearly had the highest regard for Jews. James Kirsch reports that Jung once went so far as to say "that in [Jung's] opinion, 'due to the millennia of relationship to the

Transcendental, the Jews are the Kings of the Spirit'" (1991 p.68), clearly intended as the highest accolade.

There are various accounts of Jung having helped Jews during the war. In a letter dated 19 December 1938, Jung states: "...I have a lot to do with Jewish refugees and am permanently occupied with finding a place for all my Jewish acquaintances in England and in America" (Neumann 1991 p.283).

(I) THE 'QUOTA' SYSTEM AT THE ANALYTICAL PSYCHOLOGY CLUB, ZURICH ('APC')

A dark stain in the history of the Jungian movement concerns the troubling revelation that the APC had a secret quota setting a limit on the number of Jews who were admitted as members (10%). This was unofficially in place from the 1930s, formally ratified in December 1944 and remained extant until as recently as 1950. (There was a separate category of 'guests' with a quota of 25%.)

At a workshop on the subject of these quotas in 1989 this wound still rankled, and a letter was sent by the Conference Chair of the International Association for Analytical Psychology (IAAP) about these events to the then President of the APC. It was felt that there was a need for the Club to evince some sign of atonement for these abhorrent events. Regrettably the President of the Club failed to make such a gesture by claiming that the present-day Club had no responsibility for the actions of those in positions of authority in 1933–50. Although he reassuringly stated that the Club was intending to appoint an historian to document the history of the Club, he thought it was adequate to claim the present Club membership could not be held to account for those in post in the 1940s.

As recently as 28 May 1993 John Beebe (Jungian analyst in San Francisco) and Jane Reid (Vice President of the Club) extracted an expression of regret from the Club in the form of a letter addressed to the President of the IAAP:

> There is no question that today we regret the events of that time.
> In other respects we sincerely hope – and, unfortunately, it is only a

hope – that all discrimination against anybody, especially against Jews, is a matter of the past.

(Mattoon 1996 p.714 quoted in Kirsch 2000 p.35)

(J) JUNG'S RATIONALE

Without wishing to enter into a pseudo-analysis of Jung, I would like to raise one speculative point. Could it be that Jung was searching, in Der Vaterland, for a father figure? We know from his reflections in *Memories, Dreams, Reflections* (Jaffé 1963) that he was sorely disappointed in his father. I would further posit that Switzerland as a nation is in a position of either younger sibling or child in relation to Germany. In "The Psychology of Dictatorship" (1936) Jung gushes about the Nazis: "The SS men are becoming transformed into a caste of knights" (McGuire & Hull 1977 p.92). He goes on to describe Hitler as being a "medicine man type" of dictator (ibid.). Might there be some kind of identification here? In August 1939 Jung had a dream (of which there are two recorded versions – one by Esther Harding and the other by E.A. Bennet) in which:

Hitler (who was being treated as divine and turns to Jung for advice) and Jung were placed on two corresponding mounds.

(Sherry 1991 pp.126–7)

This seems to indicate a complex identification.

Jung was deeply troubled by the events playing out across Europe. He admitted "[w]e are... much more deeply involved in the recent events in Germany than we like to admit... I had not realized how much I myself was affected" (1945a pp.194–5).

(K) APOLOGIES

Jung apologised to Leo Baeck. He also made a private apology to James Kirsch (Kirsch 1991 p.64). Jung admitted: "Any one partner in this unholy trinity [Hitler, Goebbels, Göring] should have been enough to make any man whose instincts were not warped cross himself three times" (1945a p.205).

Why these expressions of regret were not made public is a mystery and a cause for concern. Jung's reputation has suffered as a consequence. Many of the views I have cited are reprehensible and show a man who truly 'slipped up'.

SUMMARY

We have looked at Jung's outmoded formulations on race and how these have been reimagined and revised. Jung's relationship to Judaism and the Nazis has also been examined.

(2) ANIMA/ANIMUS AND FEMINIST REVISION

We turn now to looking at how feminist thinking has made a critical contribution to a modern formulation of Jung's theory of anima/animus. Jung's privileged cultural/social milieu with its roots in the 18th century mean his attitude towards both men and women is very dated and jars to the modern ear. One of the difficulties is that we come face to face with Jung's own personal complexes. In addition, one can only discuss these concepts from the vantage point of one's own gender. These personal biases need to be overcome or at least made overt. Psychology cannot be fixed; it needs to be updated.

In 1921 (Jung's earliest definition of soul as anima) he spoke of an "inner personality" (CW6 par. 803). Jung envisions: "The whole nature of man pre-supposes woman both physically and spiritually" (1945b par. 300). Jung sees this as accounting for the longings we all experience for an 'other' to 'complete' us so that we search for lovers on whom to project our unconscious needs. (This model is critiqued in the feminist accounts where the anima/animus dyad is *not* seen in terms of something missing.)

Jung then switches to a less neutral/scientific tone:

> The anima is a factor of the utmost importance in the psychology of a man wherever emotions and affects are at work. She intensifies, exaggerates, falsifies, and mythologizes all emotional relations with his work and with other people of both sexes. The resultant fantasies and entanglements are all her doing. When the anima is strongly constellated, she softens the man's character and makes him touchy, irritable, moody, jealous, vain and unadjusted.
>
> (1954 par. 144)

Elsewhere Jung continues:

This explains why it is just those very virile men who are most subject
to characteristic weaknesses; their attitude to the unconscious has
a womanish weakness and impressionability. Conversely, it is often
just the most feminine women who, in their inner lives, display an
intractability, an obstinacy, and a wilfulness that are to be found
with comparable intensity only in a man's outer attitude. These are
masculine traits which... have become qualities of her soul.

(1921 par. 804)

By 1951 (aged 76) in *Aion*, Jung makes the following highly emotive
statement:

No matter how friendly and obliging a woman's Eros may be, no logic
on earth can shake her if she is ridden by the animus. Often the man
has the feeling – and he is not altogether wrong – that only seduction or
a beating or rape would have the necessary power of persuasion.

(1951 par. 29)

Even in the 1950s this is a wholly inappropriate statement which it
is difficult to reconcile with Jung's often-stated desire to be scientific.
This compounds the myth that women are responsible for violence
upon themselves and must surely be seen in terms of Jung's own
personal complexes.

Jung sees the archetype in polarised terms:

as the anima produces *moods*, so the animus produces *opinions*; and
as the moods of a man issue from a shadowy background, so the
opinions of a woman rest on equally unconscious prior assumptions.
Animus opinions very often have the character of solid convictions
that are not lightly shaken, or of principles whose validity is seemingly
unassailable... in reality the opinions are not thought out at all.

(1945b par. 331; emphasis in original)

He continues:

In intellectual women the animus encourages a critical
disputatiousness and would-be highbrowism, which, however, consists
essentially in harping on some irrelevant weak point and nonsensically
making it the main one. Or a perfectly lucid discussion gets tangled
up in the most maddening way through the introduction of a quite
different and if possible perverse point of view. Without knowing it,
such women are solely intent upon exasperating the man and are, in
consequence, the more completely at the mercy of the animus.

(ibid. par. 335)

This partial view does not wash in the 21st century.

Jung alternately goes into poetic flights seeing women in ethereal terms, which can also be characterised as psychologically damaging to women. Both ends of this spectrum are incomplete and injurious to women.

Introducing the animus appears to be an afterthought, a counter-poise for Jung's beloved anima which, given his tendency to think in binary oppositions, he assumed:

> If, therefore, we speak of the *anima* of a man, we must logically speak of the *animus* of a woman, if we are to give the soul of a woman its right name.
>
> (1921 par. 805; emphasis in original)

Feminist scholar Naomi Goldenberg (University of Ottawa), quoted in Samuels, also disputes the symmetry of Jung's theory which she sees as an artificial construction (Samuels 1985 p.214). Douglas links this to: "Jung's tendency to organize his thinking in nineteenth century Kantian polarizations" (1990 p.54).

Jung's ideas imply that women have no soul and men have no spirit. This division creates a nonsensical split which weakens his theory and alienates some readers. Jung is always careful to balance out his theory as "though each pole is theoretically equal and no depreciation is intended, yet the comparison inevitably draws him into a socio-culturally induced hierarchy of superiority and inferiority" (Douglas 1990 p.61).

JUNG'S RELATIONSHIP WITH HIS OWN ANIMA

> I caught sight of two figures, an old man with a white beard and a beautiful, young girl.... The old man explained that he was Elijah... she called herself Salomé!... Elijah assured me that he and Salomé had belonged together from all eternity... Salomé is an anima figure. She is blind because she does not see the meaning of things. Elijah is the figure of the wise old prophet and represents the factor of intelligence and knowledge; Salomé the erotic element. One might say that the two figures are personifications of Logos and Eros.
>
> (Jaffé 1963 pp.206–7)

Jungian analyst Claire Douglas (one-time wife of J.D. Salinger), in her formidable feminist critique of Jung, wonders if Salomé's blindness is that she cannot see her potential free of the confusion of the feminine with inferiority (1990 p.70).

Jung had an ambivalent relationship to his own anima. In one breath he considers her to be "full of deep cunning" (Jaffé 1963 p.212) and in the next displays deep respect for her wisdom: "It is she who communicates the images of the unconscious to the conscious mind…. For decades I always turned to the anima" (ibid.).

Verena Kast (Jungian analyst and professor of psychology at the University of Zurich) highlights the personal dimension and Jung's mother complex:

> There are some definitions where Jung claims that the parents are the first human beings onto whom we project anima and animus (Jung 1954/1968a par. 226); thus anima and animus are influenced by these complexes, which makes them 'difficult' … *This might be the reason why Jung, at a later stage, gives a more positive meaning to anima and animus, having separated more fully from his mother and father complexes.*
>
> (Kast 2006 p.120; my emphasis)

CONFLATION OF ANIMA AND WOMEN'S PSYCHOLOGY

Conceiving of Jung's theory using a more modern approach to gender helps us to move away from the difficulties surrounding Jung's conflation of two separate ideas, that is, the notion of an anima, and the psychology of an individual woman (Hinkle 1920 p.106, Binswanger 1963, 1965, 1975, de Castillejo 1973). This is where Jung gets into problems, when he extrapolates from personal encounters with real-life women, and then makes reactive statements fired by his own personal neuroses. This is not helped by his tendency to also conflate 19th-century gender stereotypes with the notion of the anima and animus as archetypes (Kast 2006 p.116). That takes us away from anima and animus being archetypal energies.

REVISIONIST THEORY

While it can be argued that an essentialist reading of Jung is empowering for women (and Jung did encourage his own wife to become an analyst and collaborated with a number of women), a revision of Jung's theories was necessary.

Theorists have been expanding on Jung's ideas of the feminine since Harding (1955), Wolff (2011) and Emma Jung (1957) from the 1930s onwards (although Emma Jung was not as radical as the other women and was really amplifying Jung's original ideas, introducing a much-needed woman's perspective on the animus).

Claire Douglas has written an exhaustive account of Jungians concerned with the feminine, which is essential reading for any interested reader. She has an exceptionally comprehensive grasp of developments on both sides of the Atlantic. She summarises the constructive and creative work which has been done on the animus in recent decades. She elaborates: "Important extensions of theory... giving the animus both active and passive components, separating it according to stage and type, as well as separating it from a woman's own biologically masculine side" (1990 p.179). She is also concerned to rehabilitate the idea of the dark feminine, which I regard as essential in challenging the weak/inferior feminine Jung promulgates, with his conception of the anima.

Betty De Shong Meador (1984) posits a three-fold archetype of the feminine: "all aspects of which can be found in and through a woman's own body consciousness and her 'passionate bodily connection to the divine feminine...'" (Douglas 1990 p.232). She draws on the Demeter-Persephone myth, women's mysteries of initiation, and the black goddess to which she adds the red, menstruating goddess, the Tantric Dakini of sexuality (ibid.). The white goddess is symbolised by the image of the Virgin Mary; the black goddess is the underworld goddess of prophecy, divining, witches; the red goddess is the potent Yin (as in Yin and Yang) aspect of the erotic and of women's sexual power. I agree with Douglas, following Meador, when she states:

> this aspect [is] suppressed and denigrated by our culture more than any of the others; it is an essential archetype which combines the erotic, the sexual, and the spiritual in a significant and feminine way.
>
> (1990 p.232)

Verena Kast has systematically examined most of the thinkers in this field who have begun to construct a new theory of anima/animus in which both belong to men and women, which is intuitively more congruent with lived experience. Her view is that "if we start with the idea that men and women each have both an anima and an animus… [w]e are closer to the ancient Greeks' idea that spirit inspires the soul and through this interplay things are brought into being" (2006 p.116).

Building on this notion, Douglas agrees with James Hillman that this linkage must be broken:

> Further work… will undoubtedly consider the animus as separate from thinking and Logos, and define the difference. The anima/woman/feeling/Eros/Yin/relating/feminine linkage is no longer applicable, if it ever were. These concepts must be separated from each other, as much the animus/man/thinking/Logos/Yang/creating/masculine linkage…. An area of great interest to me is the role of the animus as mediator to the feeling function (Douglas 1989). Aspects of the animus that would be consistent with this but remain unexplored would be the animus as earth father, nature spirit, peace bringer, gardener, nurturer, poet, storyteller, music maker, dancer, and playful, committed lover.
>
> (1990 p.199)

Samuels (1989) argues that there is no feminine principle. He suggests that differences in feminine or masculine psychology are due to culture and society. Like Hillman, Samuels (1985) argues that "Jung's formulations of Logos and Eros and animus and anima can be stripped of their connections, not only to *sex* but to *gender*".

Young-Eisendrath and Wiedemann (1987) challenge the 'deficit model' of femininity and the internalised sense of inferiority most women experience in patriarchal society. Young-Eisendrath updates her revisions in her solo work in 1997.

There is a growing number of Jungians who question the utility of using the model of anima and animus because of the problems associated with these ideas.

GENDER

The theory of anima and animus, as well as its revised formulation, chime with contemporary notions that gender identities are more plastic than perhaps is usually granted. There has been an upsurge in 'gender bending' in recent decades as people play with identities. The current proliferation of 'trans' issues is relevant here.

Pioneering work at the interface between psychoanalysis and neuroscience is currently producing remarkable data. The neurological evidence produced by Solms and Turnbull (2002) shows that:

> in genetic terms the distinctions between the sexes are minimal and not always as clear-cut as we might imagine. Indeed our genes may show that individuals are not necessarily as unequivocally male or female as they think they are.
>
> (Maguire 2005 pp.3–20)

In the light of these scientific discoveries, Jung's ideas seem prescient.

DEAD FIDDLER

A production at the New End Theatre in Hampstead in 2006 exemplified Jung's thinking. The play – *The Dead Fiddler* by Isaac Bashevis Singer – centres on a 17-year-old woman whose body is taken over by the dybbuk (spirit) of a gypsy musician. It is as if she is possessed by him, articulating things which the young woman would never verbalise herself. 'He' is ribald and aggressive. Subsequently she also becomes possessed by the spirit of a dead prostitute who strikes up a highly animated relationship with the dead fiddler. The situation is resolved by the marriage of the two inner figures whereupon they liberate the girl by leaving her body. And this points us to the crux of the matter, that both elements in this equation – anima and animus – need to be integrated to form a fully rounded whole person.

SUMMARY

We have looked at Jung's formulation of anima-animus, how it is implicitly hierarchical, and the revisions by contemporary scholars.

---

(3) ECOPSYCHOLOGY

Many people instinctively feel touched by nature and appreciate contact with it to reconnect with their humanity. We all love to spend time by the sea, or in the woods among trees; with 'natural' things. In contrast, shopping malls can seem devoid of soul.

Jung was deeply connected to nature and spent time immersed in it both for relaxation and to develop his creativity. He carved stone and wood, 'played' with pebbles, and even built a tower in Bollingen which was his refuge where he would 'go back to nature', lighting fires for warmth and to cook. He instinctively understood that trees and stones have soul (1928 para. 295).

Ecopsychology is a discipline which has brought together the connections between the ecological and psychological. The term ecopsychology was originally coined by cultural historian Theodore Roszak (1992) although the ecology movement had started in the early 1960s. Roszak *et al's* seminal anthology (1995):

> brought together different writers and perspectives in what was already a burgeoning field of exploration and inspiration. Writers ranged from Native American perspectives on our current dislocation, to grief and despair work about environmental destruction and loss of species, to Jungians writing about the collective unconscious.
>
> (www.ecopsychology.org.uk/history, accessed 11 March 2018)

I first encountered the ecopsychology movement in 1995 when a group was formed under the auspices of Psychotherapists and Counsellors for Social Responsibility (PCSR) in the UK. At a PCSR conference in 2000 the ecopsychology group presented a stunning performance entitled "Therapists on the Titanic", which enacted the ecological crisis the world faces. It was a radical event which raised consciousness about these issues. The group worked to weave together psychology, ecology, politics and spirituality. Members of this group and others went on to write an anthology of responses to the crisis we and the planet face (Rust & Totton (Eds.) 2011).

MAN'S CONNECTION TO ANIMALS

While the ecopsychology movement is predominantly concerned with man's despoliation of the earth and our disconnection from the more-than-human world, others have been developing therapeutic approaches to working directly with animals. Man and animals have a deep and mysterious link. I have referred to the work of Rupert Sheldrake and what he calls the morphic resonance field which connects us (see Chapter 1). Animal Assisted Psychotherapy (AAT) and Equine therapy are both rapidly growing fields where therapists actually work with the animals in a session. In equine therapy the horse is seen as the therapist. The horse has remarkable intuition and hones in on a site of trauma with precision. The now departed Estonian professor of neuroscience Jaak Panksepp (1943–2017), who was Baily Endowed Chair of Animal Well-Being Science at Washington State University's College of Veterinary Medicine and emeritus Distinguished Professor in the Department of Psychology at Bowling Green State University, has demonstrated that all mammals share what he described as 'core emotional processes'. He is known for experiments with tickling rats that showed they laugh! He explored emotions with the rigour of a scientist and his *Affective Neuroscience: The Foundations of Human and Animal Emotions* (1998) is a classic in the field.

Jungian analyst Neil Russack (1936–2011) from San Francisco wrote the wonderful *Animal Guides: In Life, Myth and Dreams* (2002) in which he looks deeply at how animals come into our lives in all those realms. He explores the metaphorical meanings of animals as well as the healing power of how we can become connected to them in the sorts of ways described above.

There are therapists who allow their cats or dogs to enter into the therapy space with sometimes surprising results. The animals seem to know when the patient is in need of comfort and affection and intuitively fulfil this function in a way which the therapist cannot because of the need to abstain from [too much] physical closeness since it could potentially be seductive or misleading. The simple closeness of an animal can produce happiness and pleasure. It puts you in touch with your own instinctual/animal nature. An animal showing it likes you by being drawn to you can dispel negative feelings about yourself or of being untouchable. An anecdotal example is of my favourite 'animal therapist' Alfie (of the canine variety) who would wait at the front door for a particular patient. Even when sessions were rearranged and happened at unfamiliar times, he would be loyally waiting there for her arrival. Perhaps there are times when this is the limit of what is possible in allowing any form of intimate interaction and it can thus be a stepping stone to deeper relationships with other people.

(4) POLITICS AND ACTIVISM

The topics covered in this final chapter are political. It has been important to be transparent about the problems that exist within the Jungian field as well as looking at new developments and ways in which the field is expanding. One of these is in the realm of activism, which is controversial. Analysis is predominantly to do with interiority and looking inwards, albeit in the service of creating a better life externally in the 'real' world. Generally there is a tendency towards 'being' and not 'doing'. In recent years there has been a movement towards applying Jungian ideas in various arenas outside of the clinic. This movement has been spearheaded by Andrew Samuels (1993 and 2001) and others. The epigram on the frontispiece of his 2001 book is: "Everything starts in mysticism and ends in politics", a quote from noted French poet Charles Péguy (1873–1914), which eloquently encapsulates the arc of the journey from Jungian psychology to applying it in a political context. I mean politics here in the broadest sense although Samuels has in fact consulted to world leaders on both sides of the Atlantic. Pushing the boundaries to scrutinise theories through a contemporary political lens is important if clinical work is to remain relevant.

This activism has taken many forms such as teams of analysts travelling to locations all over Russia and Eastern Europe to bring analysis to countries where it was at one time illegal but now has thriving groups developing (Crowther & Wiener 2015). This is enhanced by the use of modern technology so that visits can be supplemented by online consultations now. Others have taken Expressive Sandwork methods (with their roots in Jungian psychology) to work with disadvantaged Palestinian children in the Middle East, to Colombia, to the Sechuan Province of China in 2008 following the earthquake in that region, and elsewhere (www.sandwork.org/).

It is to be hoped that these and other developments will keep the field of Jungian analysis and psychology alive and of relevance to young people encountering these ideas for the first time. It is a rich field to explore personally, intellectually, artistically and experimentally. Suggestions for further study may be found in the 'Further study' section at the end of the book, which includes academic institutions, reading groups (at the C.G. Jung worldwide clubs) as well as areas for more informal exploration.

SUMMARY

This closing chapter deals with various problematic, or conten-
tious, areas in the Jungian field of study which have been identified
(race, including accusations of anti-Semitism, and gender). Some of
these problems have been addressed, and some continue to need
attention. We then touched more briefly on nascent areas of interest
(ecopsychology and man's relationship with animals) which have
begun to emerge from the field and where Jungian ideas can be fruit-
fully applied.

Finally, we looked at the ways in which Jungian ideas are being
applied in the world and in politics, including a growing move
towards political activism and thinking more radically about how
Jungian psychology may be of use outside of the consulting room as
well as inside.

It is hoped that the reader's interest has been sufficiently piqued to
explore these matters further.

REFERENCES

Bair, D. (2003) *Jung: A Biography*. Boston, MA: Little Brown.

Bashevis Singer, I. (1982) "The Dead Fiddler" in *The Collected Stories of Isaac Bashevis Singer*. London: Jonathan Cape.

Binswanger, H. (1963) "Positive Aspects of the Animus" in *Spring*, 1963. Vol. 11. pp. 82–101.

Binswanger, H. (1965) "Ego, Animus and Persona in the Feminine Psyche" in *Harvest*. Vol. 11. pp. 1–14.

Binswanger, H. (1975) *Development in Modern Women's Self-Understanding*. C.G. Jung Memorial Lecture, Zurich. Unpublished manuscript, property of the Kristine Mann Library, New York.

Claremont de Castillejo, I. (1973) *Knowing Woman: A Feminine Psychology*. Boston, MA & Dorset: Shambhala Publiciations.

Cocks, G. (1991) "The Nazis and C.G. Jung" in Maidenbaum & Mitchell, 1991.

Crowther, C. & Wiener, J. (Eds.) (2015) *From Tradition to Innovation: Jungian Analysts Working in Different Cultural Settings*. Orleans, LA: Spring Journal Inc.

Dalal, F. (1988) "Jung: A Racist". *British Journal of Psychotherapy*. Vol. 4 No. 3. pp. 263–279.

Douglas, C. (1990) *The Woman in the Mirror: Analytical Psychology and the Feminine*. Boston, MA: Sigo Press.

Goldenberg, N. (1976) "A Feminist Critique of Jung" in *Signs: Journal of Women in Culture and Society* Vol.2 No.2. pp.443–449.

Harding, E. (1955) *Woman's Mysteries: Ancient and Modern. A Psychological Interpretation of the Feminine Principle as Portrayed in Myth, Story and Dreams.* London: Rider & Co, 1977.

Hinkle, B. (1923) *Recreating of the Individual: A Study of Psychological Types and their Relation to Psychoanalysis.* New York: Dodd, Mead, 1949.

Jaffé, A. (1963) *C G Jung: Memories, Dreams, Reflections.* London: Fontana Press, 1995.

Jaffé, A. (1989) "C G Jung and National Socialism" in *From the Life and Work of C. G. Jung* (Trans. R.F.C. Hull & M. Stein). Einsiedeln, Switzerland: Daimon Verlag. Also in Jung's Last Years and Other Essays. Dallas, TX: Spring Publications, 1984.

Jung, C.G. (1918) "The Role of the Unconscious" in CW 10.

Jung, C.G. (1921) *Psychological Types*, CW 6.

Jung, C.G. (1928) "The Relations between the Ego and the Unconscious" in CW 7.

Jung, C.G. (1934) "The State of Psychotherapy Today" in CW 10.

Jung, C.G. (1936) "The Psychology of Dictatorship" in McGuire & Hull, 1977

Jung, C.G. (1945a) "After the Catastrophe" in CW 10.

Jung, C.G. (1945b) "Anima and Animus" in CW 7.

Jung, C.G. (1951) *Aion*, CW 9ii.

Jung, C.G. (1954) "Concerning the Archetypes, with Special Reference to the Anima Concept" in CW 9i.

Jung, E. (1957) *Animus and Anima: Two Essays.* Putnam, CN: Spring.

Kast, V. (2006) "Anima/Animus" in *The Handbook of Jungian Psychology* (Ed. R.K. Papadopoulos). London & New York: Routledge. pp.113–129.

Kirsch, J. (1991) "Carl Gustav Jung and the Jews: The Real Story" in Maidenbaum & Martin, 1991

Kirsch, T. (2000) *The Jungians: A Comparative and Historical Perspective.* London & Philadelphia, PA: Routledge.

Maguire, M. (2005) "The Website 'Girl': Contemporary Theories about Male 'Femininity'" in *British Journal of Psychotherapy* Vol.22 No.1. pp.3–20.

Maidenbaum, A. (1991) "Lingering Shadows: A Personal Perspective" in Maidenbaum & Martin, 1991.

Maidenbaum, A. & Martin, S.A. (Eds.) (1991) *Lingering Shadows: Jungians, Freudians, and Anti-Semitism.* Boston, MA & London: Shambhala Publications Inc.

Mattoon, M.A. (Ed.) (1996) "Open Questions in Analytical Psychology" in *Proceedings of the XIIIth International Congress for Analytical Psychology in Zurich, 1995.* Einsiedeln: Daimon. p.714.

McGuire W. & Hull, R.F.C. (1977) *C.G. Jung Speaking: Interviews and Encounters.* Princeton, NJ: Princeton University Press.

Meador, B. (1984) *The Divine Feminine and Modern Woman*. (Cassette recording. Public seminar). San Francisco: The C.G. Jung Institute of San Francisco.

Neumann, M. (1991) "On the Relationship between Erich Neumann and C G Jung and the Question of Anti-Semitism" in Maidenbaum & Martin, 1991.

Panksepp, J. (1998) *Affective Neuroscience: The Foundations of Human and Animal Emotions*. Oxford & New York: Oxford University Press.

Roazen, P. (1991) "Jung and Anti-Semitism" in Maidenbaum & Martin, 1991.

Roszak, T. (Ed.) (1995) *Ecopsychology: Restoring the Earth, Healing the Mind*. San Francisco: Sierra Club Books.

Roszak, T. (1992) *The Voice of the Earth: An Exploration of Ecopsychology*. Grand Rapids, MI: Phanes Press.

Russack, N. (2002) *Animal Guides: In Life, Myth and Dreams*. Toronto: Inner City Books.

Rust, M-J. & Totton, N. (Eds) (2011) *Vital Signs: Psychological Responses to Ecological Crisis*. London: Karnac Books.

Samuels, A. (1985) *Jung and the Post-Jungians*. London & New York: Routledge.

Samuels, A. (1989) *The Plural Psyche*. London & New York: Routledge.

Samuels, A. (1991) "National Socialism, National Psychology and Analytical Psychology" in Maidenbaum & Martin, 1991.

Samuels, A. (1993) *The Political Psyche*. London & New York: Routledge.

Samuels, A. (2001) *Politics on the Couch: Citizenship and the Internal Life*. London: Profile Books.

Sherry, J. (1991) "The Case of Jung's Alleged Anti-Semitism" in Maidenbaum & Martin, 1991.

Solms, M. & Turnbull. O. (2002) *The Brain and the Inner World: An Introduction to the Neuroscience of Subjective Experience*. New York: Other Press

Vannoy Adams, M. and Sherry, J. (1991) "Significant Words and Events" in Maidenbaum & Martin, 1991.

Wolff, T. (2011) *Essays on Analytical Psychology*. Einsiedeln: Daimon Verlag.

Young-Eisendrath, P. & Wiedemann, F. (1987) *Female Authority: Empowering Women through Psychotherapy*. New York: Guilford.

Young-Eisendrath, P. (1997) "Gender and Contrasexuality: Jung's Contribution and Beyond" in *The Cambridge Companion to Jung* (Ed. P. Young-Eisendrath & T. Dawson). Cambridge: Cambridge University Press. pp. 223–239.

BIBLIOGRAPHY

ON RACE

Dalal, F. (2012) *Thought Paralysis: The Virtues of Discrimination*. London: Karnac Books.

Davids, F. (2011) *Internal Racism: A Psychoanalytic Approach to Race and Difference*. Basingstoke, Hampshire & New York: Palgrave Macmillan.

Fanon, F. (2008 [1952]) *Black Skins, White Masks*. New York: Grove Press.

Hirsch, A. (2018) *Brit(ish): On Race Identity and Belonging*. London: Jonathan Cape.

Lowe, F. (Ed.) (2014) *Thinking Space: Promoting Thinking about Race, Culture and Diversity in Psychotherapy and Beyond*. London: Karnac Books.

ON GENDER

Butler, J. (2006) *Gender Trouble* (Routledge Classics). New York & Abingdon, Oxon: Routledge.

de Beauvoir, S. (1997 [1949]) *The Second Sex* (Vintage Classics). London: Vintage.

Orbach, S. (1988) *Fat is a Feminist Issue*. London: Arrow Books.

Wolf, N. (2012) *Vagina: A New Biography*. London: Virago.

ON GENDER AND RACE

hooks, b. & Hall, S. (2017) *Uncut Funk: A Contemplative Dialogue*. London & New York: Routledge.

ON ECOPSYCHOLOGY

Bernstein, J. (2006) *Living in the Borderland: The Evolution of Consciousness and the Challenge of Healing Trauma*. London & New York: Routledge.

Buzzell, L. & Chalquist, C. (2009) *Ecotherapy: Healing with Nature in Mind*. San Francisco: Sierra Club Books.

Macy, J. (1991) *World as Lover, World as Self*. Berkeley, NC: Parallax Press.

Roszak, T. *et al.* (Eds.) (1995) *Ecopsychology: Restoring the Earth, Healing the Mind*. Berkeley, NC: Sierra Club Books.

RESOURCES

Climate Psychology Alliance: www.climatepsychologyalliance.org/

Excellent website with resources, history of movement and links: www.ecopsychology.org.uk/

The Eden Project: www.edenproject.com/

The Findhorn Foundation: www.findhorn.org/

The Fawcett Society is the UK's leading charity campaigning for gender equality since 1866: www.fawcettsociety.org.uk/

International Community for Ecopsychology: www.ecopsychology.org/

International Association for Expressive Sandwork: www.sandwork.org

LEAP equine psychotherapy facility: www.leapequine.com/

Politics & Psychotherapy International (Wiley Blackwell), which is the official journal of Psychotherapists and Counsellors for Social Responsibility. Web: www.pcsr.org.uk.

Resurgence & Ecologist is a magazine tied to Schumacher College in the UK: www.resurgence.org/

Society for Companion Animal Studies: www.scas.org.uk/

FURTHER READING

Memories, Dreams, Reflections by C.G. Jung (recorded and edited by Aniela Jaffé)
Man and His Symbols (conceived and edited by C.G. Jung)
The Undiscovered Self: C.G. Jung answers questions raised by the present world
   crisis.

LIST OF VOLUMES IN THE COLLECTED WORKS OF C.G. JUNG

(Edited by Sir Herbert Read, Michael Fordham MD, MRCP, and Gerhard Adler,
   PhD; Trans. by R.F.C. Hull.)

Volume 1	*Psychiatric Studies*
Volume 2	*Experimental Researches*
Volume 3	*The Psychogenesis of Mental Disease*
Volume 4	*Freud and Psychoanalysis*
Volume 5	*Symbols of Transformation*
Volume 6	*Psychological Types*
Volume 7	*Two Essays on Analytical Psychology*
Volume 8	*The Structure and Dynamics of the Psyche*
Volume 9i	*The Archetypes and the Collective Unconscious*
Volume 9ii	*Aion*
Volume 10	*Civilization in Transition*
Volume 11	*Psychology and Religion: West and East*

SUPPLEMENTARY VOLUMES TO THE COLLECTED WORKS:

The Zofingia Lectures
Analytical Psychology: Notes on the Seminar Given in 1925
Dream Analysis: Notes on the Seminar Given in 1928–30

Visions: Notes of the Seminar Given in 1930–34 (two volumes)

The Psychology of Kundalini Yoga: Notes of the Seminar Given in 1932
Nietzche's Zarathustra: Notes of the Seminar Given in 1934–9 (two volumes)

The following have subsequently been published by The Philemon Foundation who aim to publish the complete works of C.G. Jung:

The Red Book: Liber Novus

The Red Book: Reader's Edition
A text edition, containing the complete text, introduction and scholarly apparatus but minus the images.

The Jung-White Letters

Jung Contra Freud: The 1912 New York Lectures on the Theory of Psychoanalysis.
Originally published in Jung's Collected Works, Volume 4. This edition features a historical contextual introduction by Sonu Shamdasani.

The Question of Psychological Types: The Correspondence of C. G. Jung and Hans Schmid-Guisan 1915–1916

Introduction to Jungian Psychology: Notes on the Seminar on Analytical Psychology Given in 1925

Children's Dreams: Notes on the Seminar Given in 1936–40

Dream Interpretation Ancient & Modern: Notes from the Seminar Given in 1936–41
Analytical Psychology in Exile: The Correspondence of C.G. Jung and Erich
Neumann

On Psychological and Visionary Art: Notes from C. G. Jung's Lecture on Gérard
de Nerval's Aurélia
C. G. Jung and Adolf Keller: A Conversation Between Psychology and Theology
The History of Modern Psychology: Lectures Delivered at the ETH Zurich,
Volume 1, 1933–4

This is an evolving list. See: http://philemonfoundation.org/about-philemon/
about-the-foundation/

You might also be interested in:

Uniform Edition of the Writings of James Hillman (1926–2011), the founder
of Archetypal Psychology. The uniform, clothbound set of 11 volumes of the
writings of James Hillman (also available as ebooks) unites major lectures,
occasional writings, scholarly essays, clinical papers and interviews – arranged
thematically.

See: www.springpublications.com/uniformedition.html

Bair, D. (2004) *Jung: A Biography*. London: Little Brown.

Bishop, P. (1999) *Jung in Contexts: A Reader*. London & New York: Routledge.

Goss, P. (2015) *Jung: A Complete Introduction*. London: John Murray Learning.

Shamdasani, S. (2003) *Jung and the Making of Modern Psychology: The Dream of a
Science*. Cambridge: Cambridge University Press.

McLynn, F. (1996) *Carl Gustav Jung: A Biography*. London: Bantam Press.

Stevens, A. (1990) *On Jung*. Princeton, NJ: Princeton University Press.

Storr, A. (1983) *The Essential Jung: Selected Writings*. Princeton, NJ: Princeton
University Press.

Tacey, D. (2006) *How to Read Jung*. London: Granta Books.

Wilmer, H.A. (2013) *Practical Jung: Nuts and Bolts of Jungian Psychotherapy*.
Wilmette, IL: Chiron Publications.

Wilmer, H.A. (2013) *Understandable Jung: The Personal Side of Jungian Psychology*.
Wilmette, IL: Chiron Publications.

FURTHER STUDY

The International Association for Analytical Psychology (which is the
umbrella body for Jungian analysts worldwide): www.iaap.org/ was founded
in 1955 by a group of psychoanalysts to sustain and promote the work of C.G.
Jung. It is the accrediting and regulatory organisation for all professional analytical psychologist groups. Today the IAAP recognises 58 groups and societies

throughout the world, and over 3,000 analysts trained in accordance with standards established by the Association. Training institutes worldwide may be found listed on their website.

Department for Psychosocial and Psychoanalytic Studies (formerly the Centre for Psychoanalytic Studies)

University of Essex

Wivenhoe Park

Colchester

Essex CO4 3SQ

UK

+44 (0) 1206 873333

enquiries@essex.ac.uk

www.essex.ac.uk/cps/about/

Undergraduate, postgraduate and doctoral study in depth psychology.

Drawing on research excellence, the Centre offers a wide range of undergraduate and postgraduate courses and research opportunities in both psychoanalytic and Jungian thought. At Essex you are taught and supervised by senior clinicians and world-class scholars.

Distance learning is allowed.

Pacifica Graduate Institute

249 Lambert Road

Carpinteria

California 93013

Telephone: 805.969.3626

www.pacifica.edu/

Pacifica Graduate Institute is an accredited graduate school offering masters and doctoral degree programmes framed in the traditions in depth psychology.

Distance learning is allowed.

Birkbeck

Malet St, Bloomsbury, London WC1E 7HX

Bloomsbury

London WC1E 7HX

UK

www.bbk.ac.uk/study/2017/postgraduate/programmes/TMSPDHDV_C/

Psychodynamics of Human Development (MSc). Run in collaboration with the British Psychotherapy Foundation (BPF)

USEFUL WEBSITES

ARAS (Archive for Research in Archetypal Symbolism): http://aras.org/
Treasure-trove resource for exploring images. It contains photographic images, each cross-indexed, individually mounted, and accompanied by scholarly commentary. The commentary includes a description of the image with a cultural history that serves to place it in its unique historical and geographical setting. Often it also includes an archetypal commentary that brings the image into focus for its modern psychological and symbolic meaning, as well as a bibliography for related reading and a glossary of technical terms.

See their *The Book Of Symbols: Reflections On Archetypal Images.* Köln: Taschen, 2010.

C.G. Jung Page: www.cgjungpage.org/
Begun in 1995, The Jung Page provides online educational resources for the Jungian community around the world. With the cooperation and generosity of analysts, academics, independent scholars and commentators, and the editors of several Jungian journals, The Jung Page provides a place to encounter innovative writers and to enter into a rich, on-going conversation about psychology and culture. The Jung Page is hosted and edited by The Jung Center of Houston.

International Association for Jungian Studies: www.jungianstudies.org/index.php
The IAJS exists to promote and develop Jungian and post-Jungian Studies and scholarship on an international basis.

International Association for the Study of Dreams: www.asdreams.org/

There are C.G. Jung Clubs around the world. The first was opened in 1916 in Zurich: www.psychologyclub.ch/en/cg-jung

C.G. Jung Club, London: www.jungclub-london.org/
The Club was founded in 1922 by close associates of C.G. Jung and ever since has continued to keep alive the feeling of community shared by those with experience of Jungian analysis and those interested in the work of Jung.

C.G. Jung Club of Orange County, California: www.junginoc.org/home.htm
The Club was established in 1974. Its purpose is to promote an interest in, and understanding of, Jungian Psychology, and to cultivate a collegial environment in which participants can experience personal development and growth.

Analytical Psychology Club of New York: http://jungclubnyc.org/
Formed in 1936, its purpose is to provide a gathering place for self-discovery.

The Guild of Pastoral Psychology: www.guildofpastoralpsychology.org.uk/index.php/about-us/the-guild
The Guild of Pastoral Psychology (based in the UK) offers a rich forum for anyone interested in understanding the relationship between spirituality, religion and depth psychology, with particular reference to the work and writings of C.G. Jung. The Guild was founded in 1937, with Jung as its Patron.

INDEX

Made in United States
North Haven, CT
26 December 2023

46603070R00127